Tom Ridgway
Oct 03

Ronald Searle

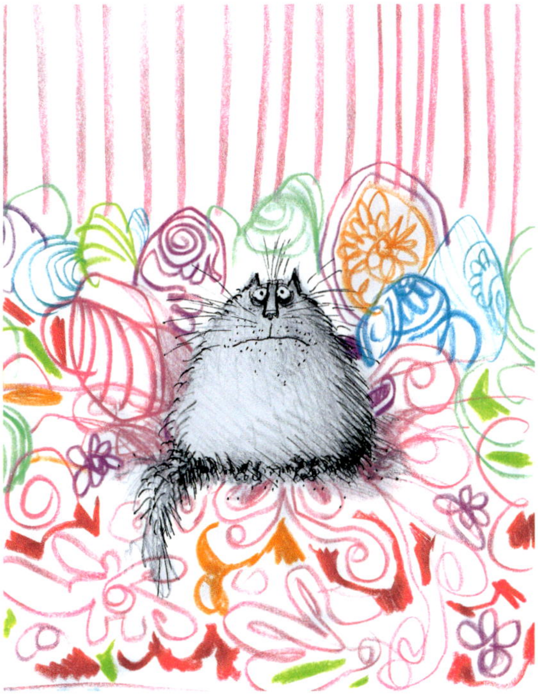

Chris Beetles
2003

If compliments, congratulations, felicitations and laurels are to be showered on the occasion of this exotic display, they should be entirely directed onto the head of Chris Beetles. He alone was the hunter-gatherer. This is his collection, his choice, his exhibition. I, the perpetrator, have left it all to him. I do not know what is being shown, which effectively prevents me from tearing much of it up and jumping on it. Meanwhile I wish him all the success in the world.

Ronald Searle

August 2003

RONALD SEARLE

Ronald William Fordham Searle, AGI NS (born 1920)

The son of a railwayman, Ronald Searle was born in Cambridge on 3 March 1920, and was educated in the town at the Boys' Central School. He started work as a solicitor's clerk, then joined the hire purchase department of the Co-operative Society, studying in the evenings and later full-time at Cambridge Technical College and School of Art (1935-39).
He contributed cartoons regularly to the *Cambridge Daily News* from the age of fifteen. Enlisting in the Royal Engineers at the outbreak of the Second World War, he spent some time in Kirkcudbright, where he encountered evacuees from St Trinnean's, a progressive girls' school situated in Edinburgh. This resulted in his first cartoon for *Lilliput*, published in October 1941, and later developed into one of his most famous creations, through a series of books and their cinematic spin-offs. He first saw a copy of the *Lilliput* cartoon only in 1942, while incarcerated at Changi Camp, Singapore as a Japanese prisoner-of-war. Remarkably, he survived the horrific experiences of both imprisonment and slave labour and managed to produce a visual record of life in the prison camp. On his return to England in 1945, he exhibited the surviving pictures at the Cambridge School of Art and, in the following year, published *Forty Drawings*. The exhibition and volume together established his reputation as one of Britain's most powerful draughtsmen, and led to several opportunities to record the atmosphere of post-war Europe. His familiarly audacious style was equally developed through his early contributions to *Punch* and crystallised in his comic collection, *The Female Approach* (1949), which was highly praised by Max Beerbohm. Throughout the fifties, he produced a large variety of illustrations which together seemed to present a guide to life in Britain. In *Punch* alone, 'Heroes of Our Time', such as T S Eliot, rubbed shoulders with teddy boys and other inhabitants of 'The Big City'. Such was his success that his rejection of family and country in a move to Paris in 1961 came as a great surprise. However, it offered a fresh start, resulting in several solo shows, including major exhibitions at the prestigious institutions of the Bibliothèque Nationale, Paris, the Berlin-Dahlem Museum and the Wilhelm-Busch-Museum, Hanover. He also reached a new audience with his contributions to film and television, most notably *Those Magnificent Men in their Flying Machines* (1965). Now remarried and living in rural France, Searle continues to work to his own uncompromising standard. More recent titles include: *Ronald Searle's Big Fat Cat Book* (1982), *The Illustrated Winespeak* (1983), *Ronald Searle's Non-Sexist Dictionary* (1988), *Slightly Foxed – But Still Desirable* (1989), *The Tales of Grandpa Cat* (1994) and *Ronald Searle in Le Monde* (2002). Notable exhibitions include two at the Wilhelm-Busch-Museum: a large retrospective (1996) and a joint exhibition with his jeweller wife, Monica (2001-2002).

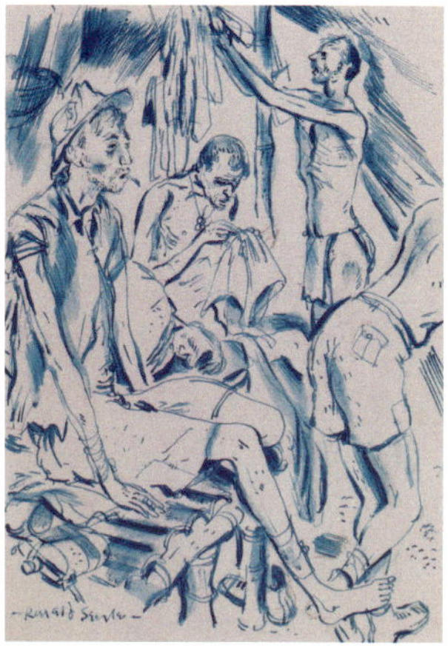

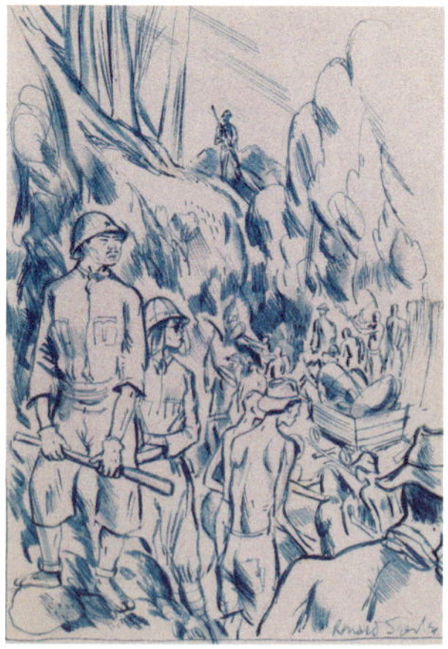

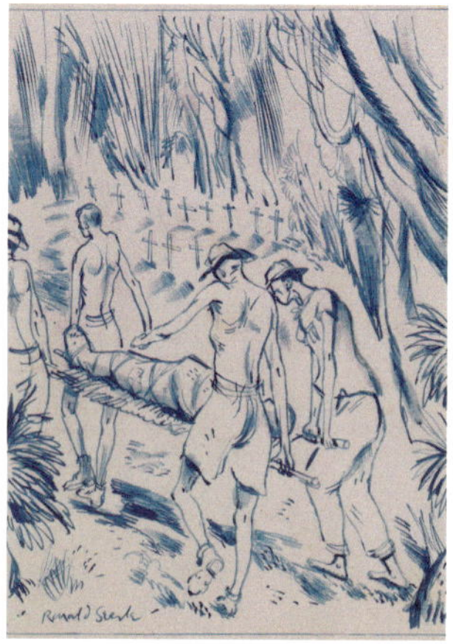

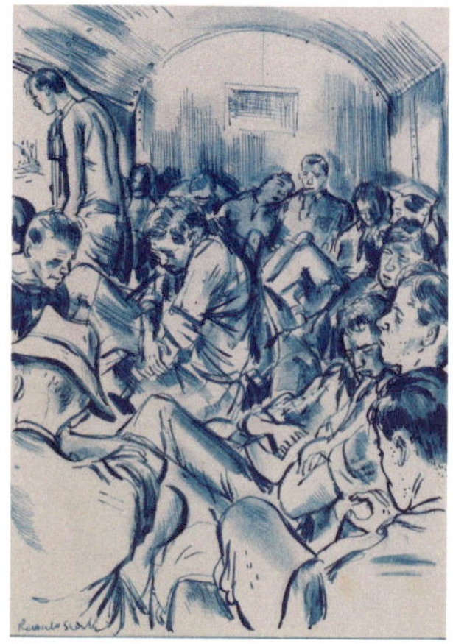

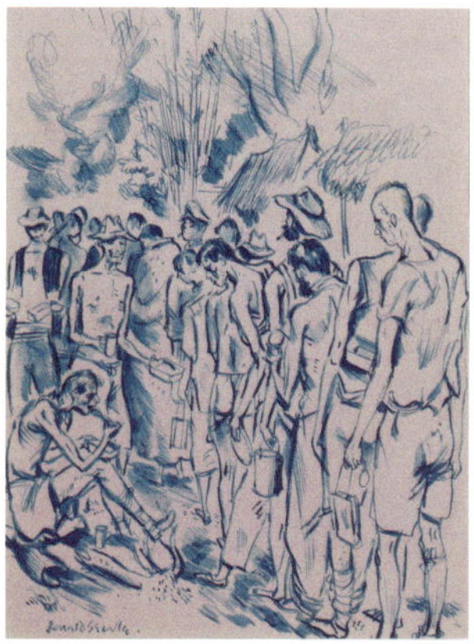

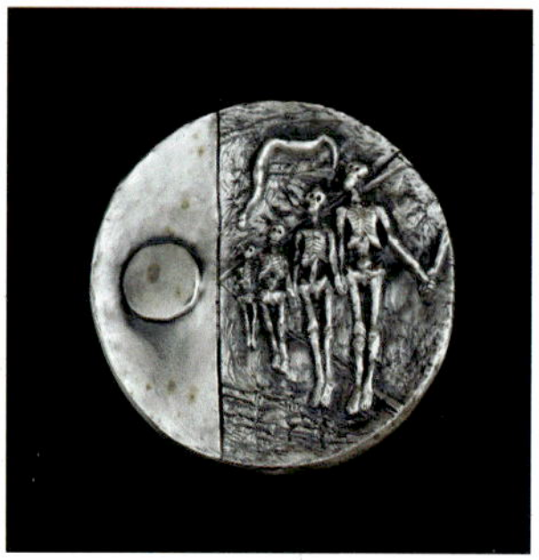

Front

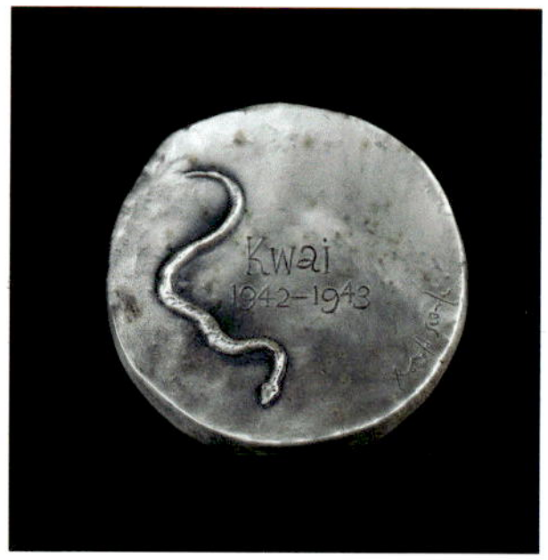

Reverse

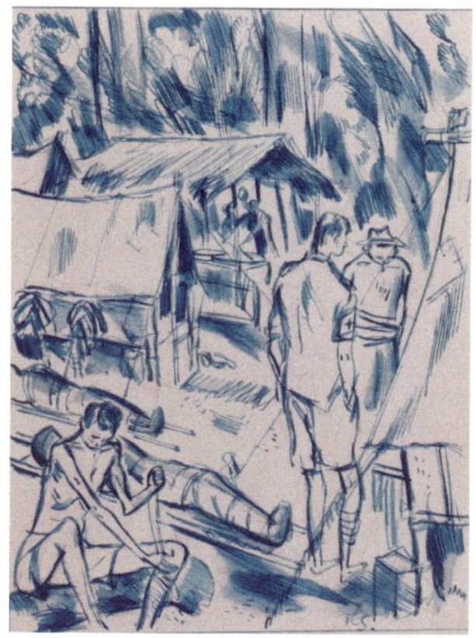

1 TENT LIFE
AND EMACIATION
signed and inscribed with title
pen and ink on tinted paper
6 ½ x 4 ½ inches

2 THE MEAL QUEUE
signed and inscribed with title
pen and ink on tinted paper
7 x 5 inches

3 ROCK BREAKING
signed
pen and ink on tinted paper
6 ¾ x 5 inches

5 A BURIAL
signed and inscribed with title
pen and ink on tinted paper
6 ¾ x 4 ¾ inches

4 KWAI 50TH
ANNIVERSARY MEDAL
signed and inscribed 'Kwai
1942-1943' on reverse
bronze
2 ¾ inches diameter
Cast in 1991

6 FREIGHT TRAIN
TO THAILAND
signed and inscribed with title
pen and ink on tinted paper
6 ¾ x 4 ¾ inches

7 SICK BAY
signed and inscribed with title
pen and ink on tinted paper
6 ½ x 4 ¾ inches

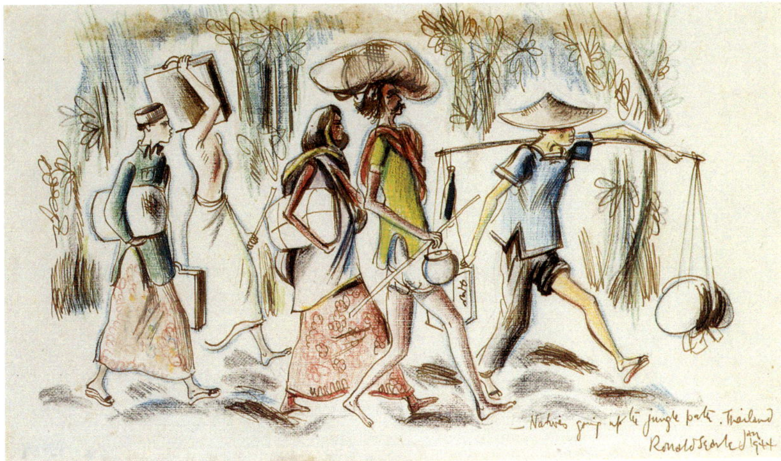

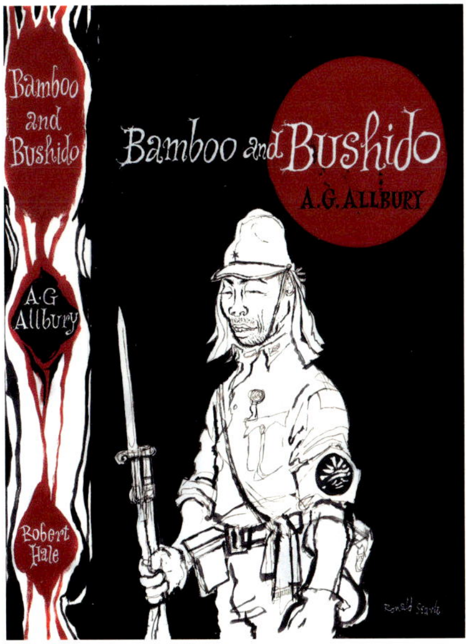

8 BAMBOO AND BUSHIDO
signed
pen ink, watercolour and bodycolour
15 x 11 ¾ inches

Illustrated: A G Allbury, *Bamboo and Bushido*, London: Robert Hale, 1955, dustjacket

9 NATIVES GOING UP THE JUNGLE PATH, THAILAND
signed, inscribed with title and dated 'Jan 1944'
pen ink and coloured pencil
4 ½ x 7 ¾ inches

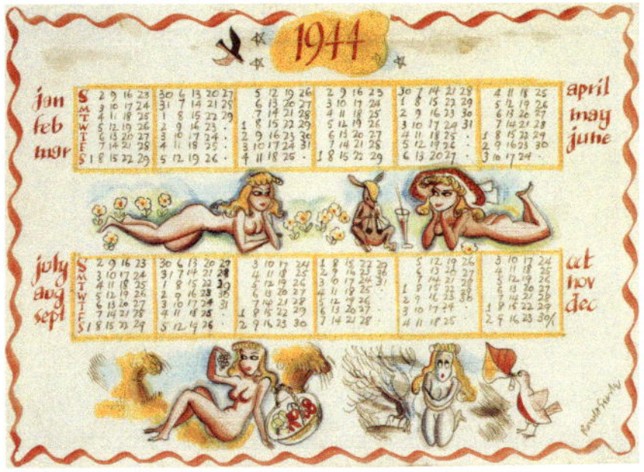

10 CALENDAR FOR 1944
signed
pen and ink
5 ½ x 8 inches

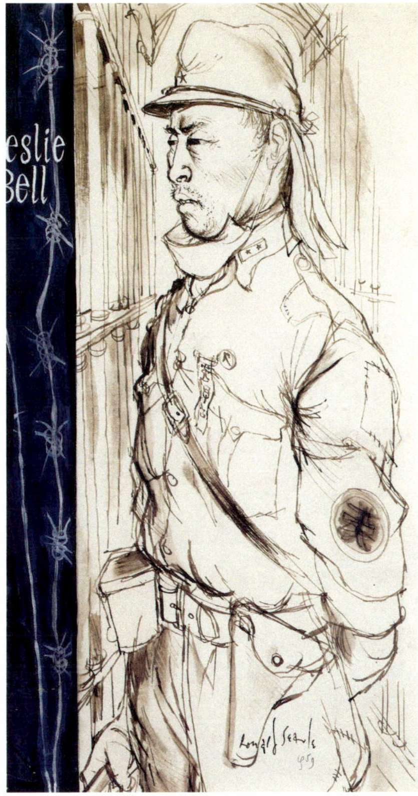

11 DESTINED MEETING
signed and dated 1959
pen ink and monochrome watercolour
11 ¾ x 6 ½ inches

Illustrated: Leslie Bell, *Destined Meeting*, London: Odhams Press, 1959, dustjacket

Exhibited: 'The Artists of the Radio Times', Chris Beetles Ltd, September 2002, no 134

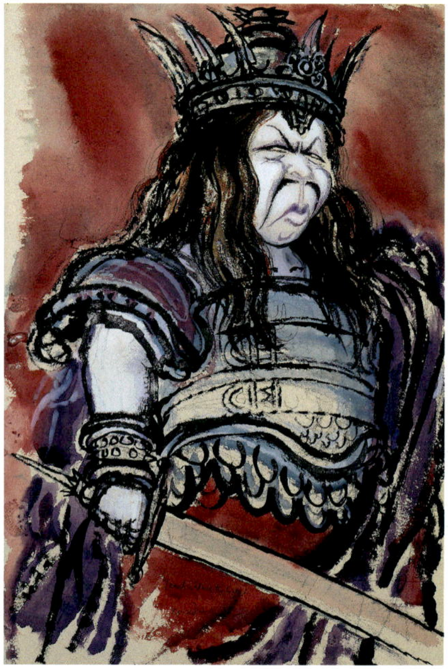

12 DONALD WOLFIT AS TAMBURLAINE THE GREAT
signed, inscribed 'Tamberlaine the Great' and dated 1954
pen ink and watercolour with bodycolour on tinted paper
21 ½ x 15 inches

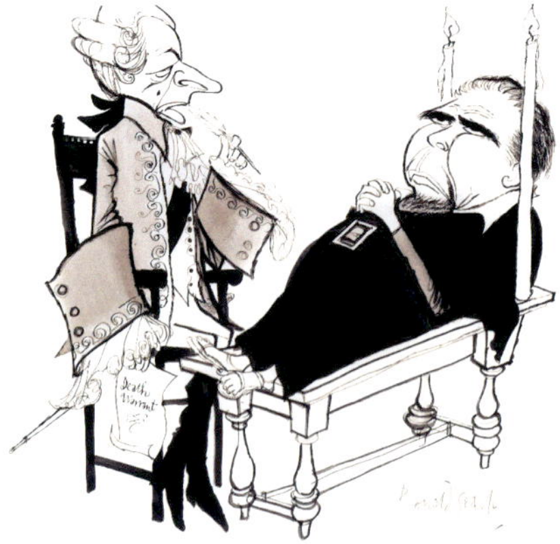

13 PUNCH THEATRE
[THE STRONG ARE LONELY]
DON PEDRO DE MIURA...ROBERT HARRIS
ALFONSO FERNANDEZ...DONALD WOLFIT
signed and inscribed with title
pen ink and monochrome watercolour
14 ¼ x 16 ¼ inches
Illustrated: *Punch*, 30 November 1955, page 644 (a review by Eric Keown of *The Strong are Lonely* by Fritz Hochwalder at the Piccadilly Theatre)

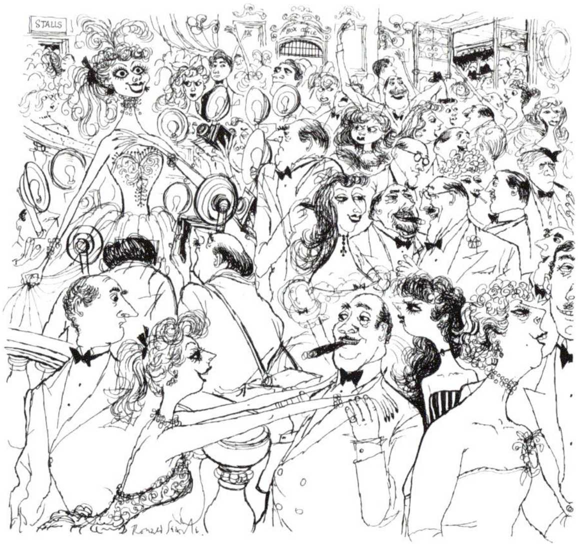

14 THE FIRST NIGHT SCENE
signed, inscribed with title below mount
inscribed with publishing details and dated 1952 on reverse
pen and ink; 10 ½ x 12 inches
Illustrated: *Punch*, 23 April 1952, page 520, 'At the Theatre';
Christopher Fry, *An Experience of Critics*, London: Perpetua, 1952, page 59, 'Who's Who Among the Critics'

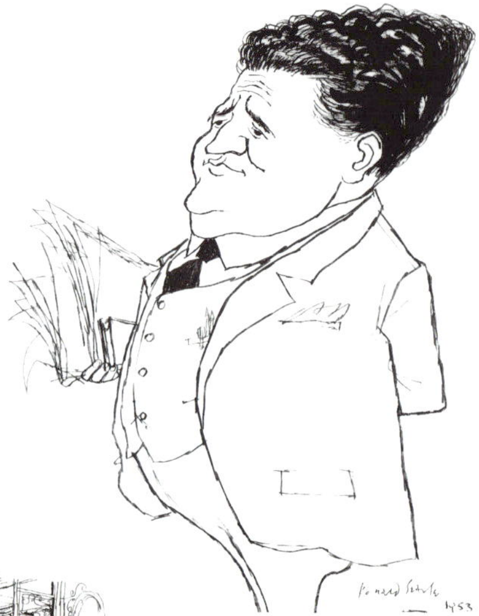

15 ALAN DENT
signed
inscribed 'Alan Dent – the Critic at the Theatre as seen by' and dated 1953 by another hand
pen and ink
11 x 8 ½ inches
Illustrated: Christopher Fry, *An Experience of Critics*, London: Perpetua, 1952, page 43

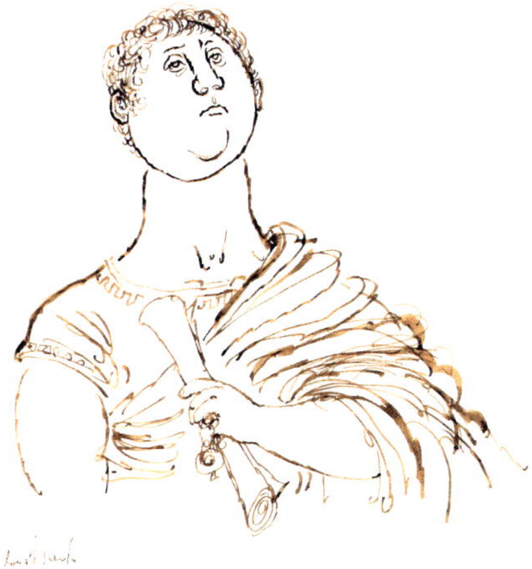

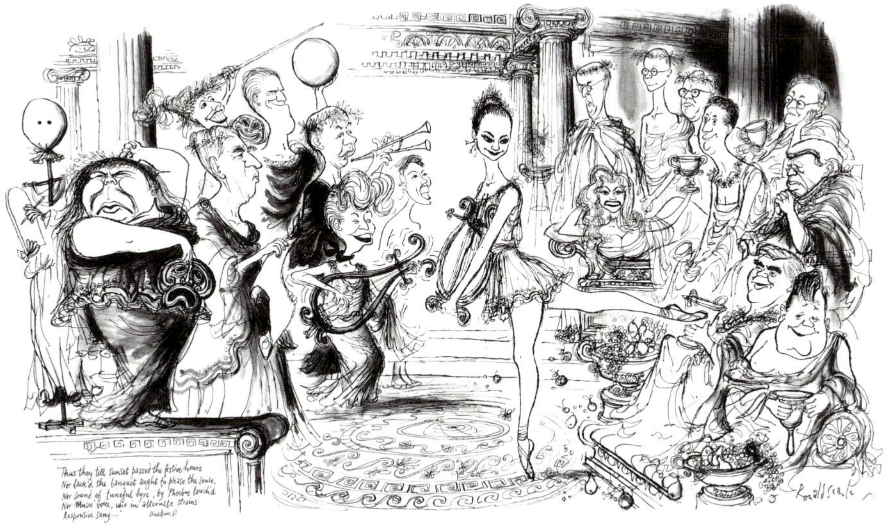

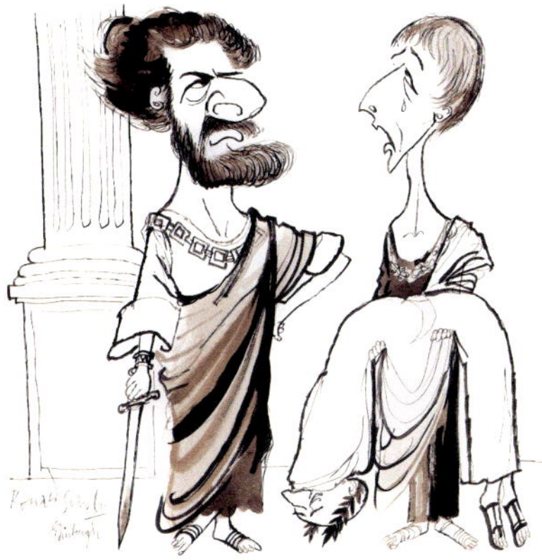

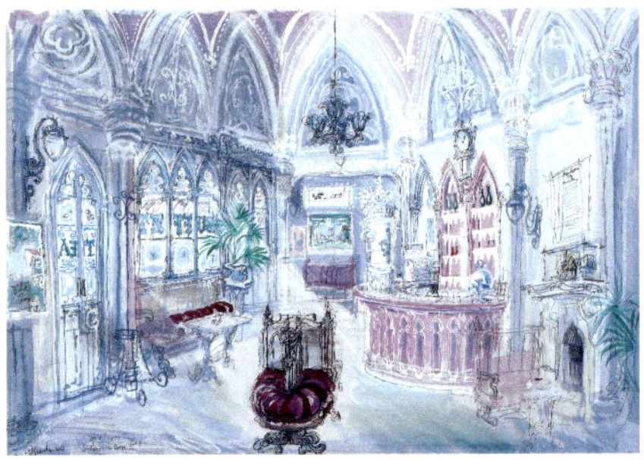

16 JULIUS CAESAR
signed
pen and ink
8 ¼ x 7 ½ inches

Illustrated: Christopher Fry, *A Phoenix too Frequent*, London: Oxford University Press, 1959, page 4

17 JULIUS CAESAR
BRUTUS...PAUL ROGERS,
MARC ANTONY...JOHN NEVILLE
PUNCH THEATRE, EDINBURGH FESTIVAL
signed and inscribed with title and 'Edinburgh'
pen and ink; 14 ½ x 16 inches

[17 cont.]
Illustrated: *Punch*, 31 August 1955, page 254 (a review by Eric Keown of *Julius Caesar* by William Shakespeare performed by the Old Vic Company at the Edinburgh Festival)

18 'WILD THYME'
ST PANDORA CROSS – ACT 1
signed, inscribed with title and dated 1955
inscribed with title below mount
pen ink, watercolour and bodycolour
17 x 24 ½ inches

19 THE MODERN OLYMPUS. THE GODS BEING ENTERTAINED BY THE MUSES
signed
inscribed with title, publishing details and dated 1957 on reverse
pen ink and monochrome watercolour
18 x 29 ¾ inches

Illustrated: *Punch*, 27 November 1957, pages 628 and 629

Key: left to right, with the last four figures reading downwards:

The Muses

Calliope (Epic Poetry)	Situation Vacant
Melpomene (Tragedy)	Sir Donald Wolfit
Thalia (Comedy)	Joyce Grenfell
Clio (History)	Arnold Toynbee
Urania (Astronomy)	The Astronomer Royal
Euterpe (Lyric Poetry)	John Betjeman
Erato (Erotic Poetry)	Tommy Steele
Polyhymnia (Sublime Hymns)	Vera Lynn
Terpsichore (The Dance)	Dame Margot Fonteyn

The Gods

The Church	The Archbishop of Canterbury
Pulchritude	Sabrina
Education	Sir John Wolfenden
The Trades Unions	Frank Cousins
The Press	Sir William Haley
Science	Sir William Penney
The Law	Lord Goddard
Politics	Aneurin Bevan
Campanology	Lord Hailsham

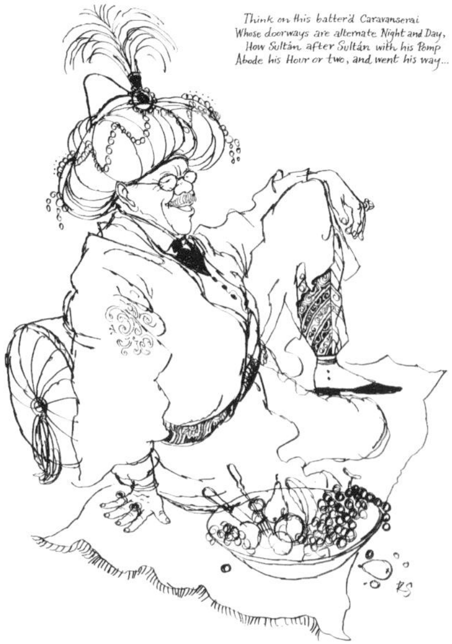

20 THINK ON THIS BATTER'D CARAVANSERAI / WHOSE DOORWAYS ARE ALTERNATE NIGHT AND DAY / HOW SULTAN AFTER SULTAN WITH HIS POMP / ABODE HIS HOUR OR TWO, AND WENT HIS WAY...
signed with initials and inscribed with title
pen and ink
13 x 9 ½ inches

This is a portrait of R Lawrence Marsh, the President of the Omar Khayyam Club in 1953

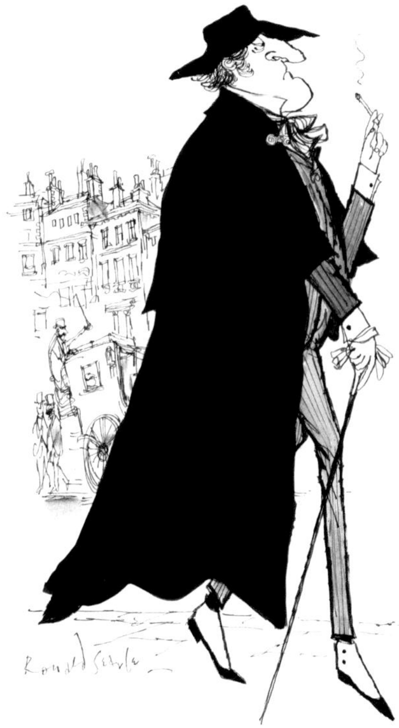

21 THE ACTOR-MANAGER
signed, inscribed with title and 'Londoners of the 'nineties' and dated 1956
inscribed with title on reverse
pen ink and monochrome watercolour
14 ¼ x 9 ¾ inches

Illustrated: *Mr Rothman's New Guide to London. Together with a Guide to some Londoners of the Eighteen-Nineties*, London: Rothman's of Pall Mall, 1958, page 46

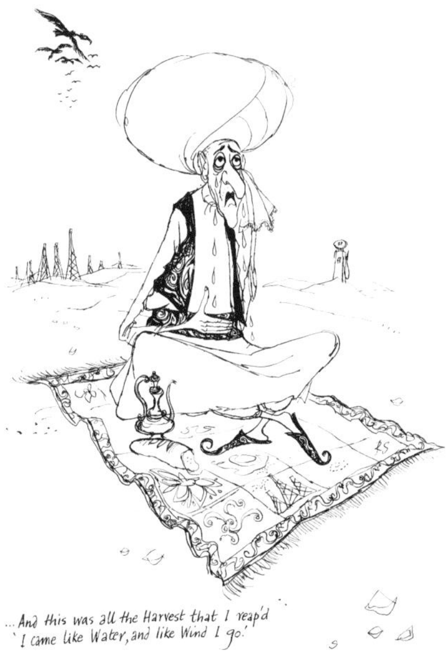

22 ...AND THIS WAS ALL THE HARVEST THAT I REAP'D
'I CAME LIKE WATER, AND LIKE WIND I GO.'
signed with initials and inscribed with title
pen and ink
12 ¾ x 9 inches

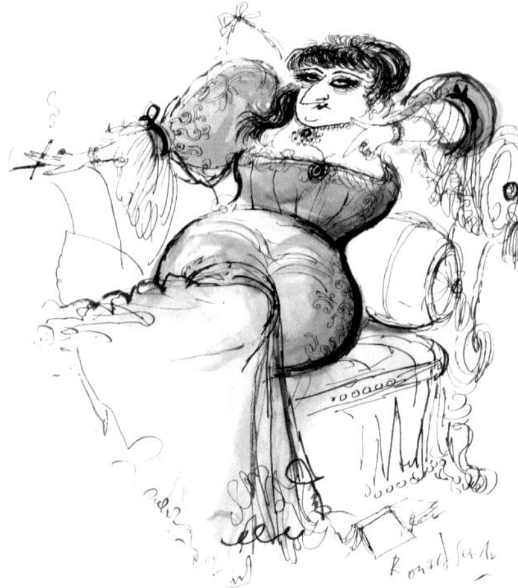

23 THE TRAGEDY QUEEN
signed, inscribed with title and 'Londoners of the 'nineties' and dated 1956
pen ink and monochrome watercolour
14 ½ x 12 ¾ inches

Illustrated: *Mr Rothman's New Guide to London. Together with a Guide to some Londoners of the Eighteen-Nineties*, London: Rothman's of Pall Mall, 1958, page 10

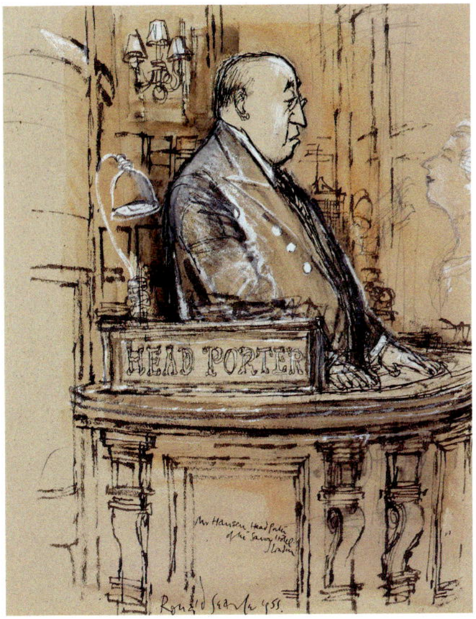

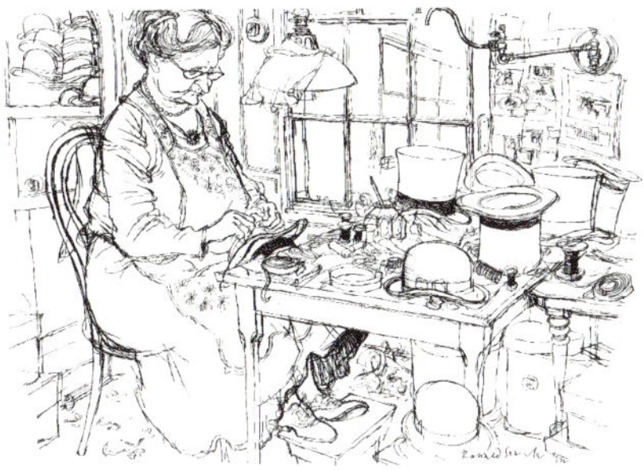

24 MR HANSEN, HEAD PORTER OF THE SAVOY HOTEL, LONDON
signed, inscribed with title and dated 1955
inscribed 'John Hansen, Head Porter of the Savoy Hotel controls the staff of porters and doormen from his cubby hole between the revolving doors. He has six telephones on his desk.' below mount
pen ink and bodycolour with pencil on tinted paper
12 x 9 ¾ inches

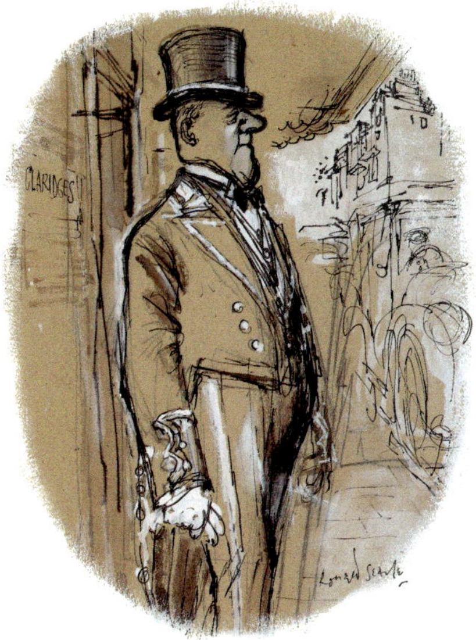

25 MISS JENNINGS: TWO THOUSAND THIMBLES WORN OUT IN THE INTERESTS OF MALE VANITY
signed, inscribed with title and 'London Characters: top hat repairer at Lock's, St James Street' and dated 1952
pen and ink
11 x 14 ½ inches

Illustrated: *News Chronicle*, 15 May 1953, page 6
Ronald Searle and Kaye Webb, *Looking at London*, London: News Chronicle, 1953, page 71

26 JACK WARBURTON, CARRIAGE MAN AT CLARIDGES HOTEL HAS SALUTED MORE KINGS THAN MANY PRIME MINISTERS. TOP HAT, BLACK TIE AND TAILS.
signed
inscribed with title below mount
pen ink and bodycolour on tinted paper
11 x 9 inches

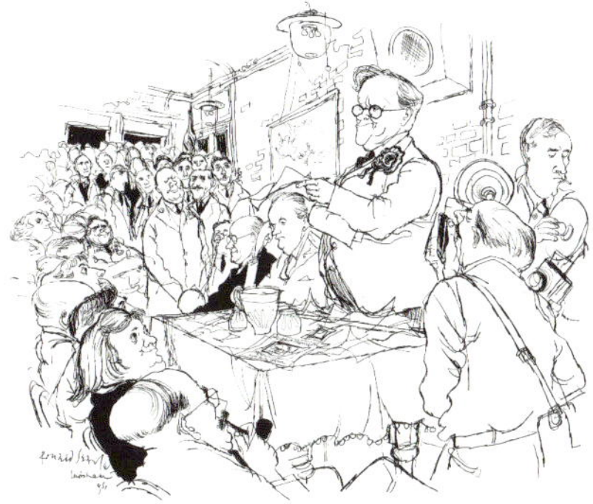

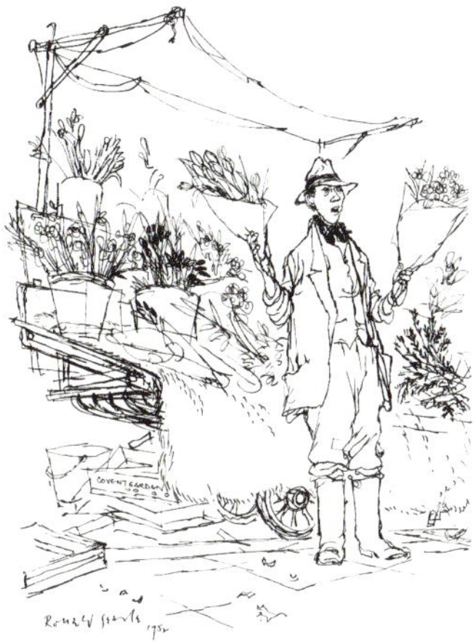

27 ON THE ROAD: HERBERT MORRISON ELECTIONEERING
signed, inscribed 'Lewisham' and dated 1951
pen and ink
13 ½ x 14 inches

Illustrated: *News Chronicle*, 18 October 1951

28 FLOWER SELLER, KING'S ROAD, CHELSEA
signed and dated 1952
inscribed with title, publishing details and dated 1952 on reverse
pen and ink
9 x 6 ½ inches

Illustrated: Ronald Searle and Kaye Webb, *Looking at London*, London: News Chronicle, 1953, frontispiece

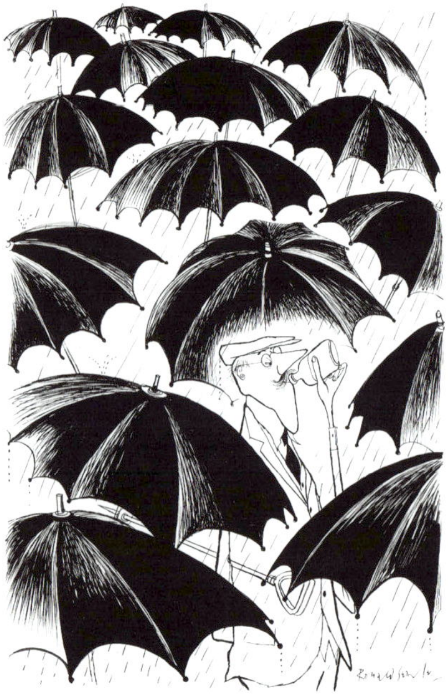

29 HAVE A GOOD RUM FOR YOUR MONEY
signed
pen and ink
15 x 10 inches
Designed as advertising for Lemon Hart Rum, 1950s

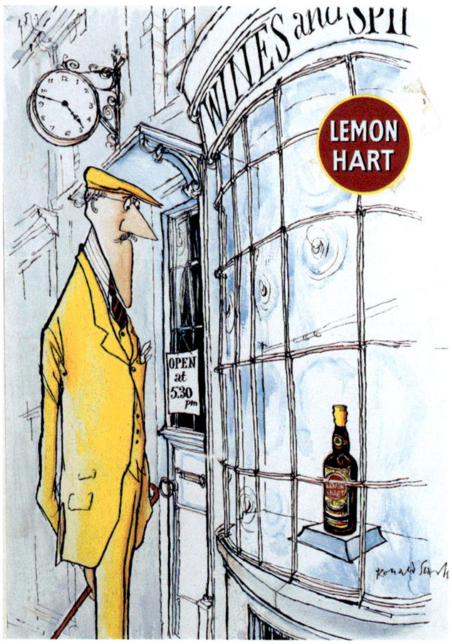

30 HAVE A GOOD RUM FOR YOUR MONEY
signed
indistinctly inscribed with title below mount
pen ink, watercolour and bodycolour
17 ½ x 11 ¾ inches
Designed as advertising for Lemon Hart Rum, 1950s

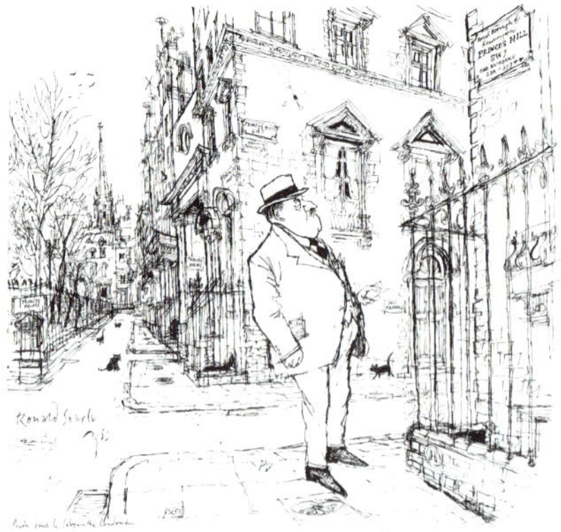

31 PERDU DANS LE LABYRINTHE LONDONIEN...
signed, inscribed with title, 'M. Pocket lost', publishing details and dated 1955
pen and ink
12 x 13 ½ inches
Illustrated: *Figaro*, Paris, 18 February 1955, 'England and the English' by Pierre Daninos

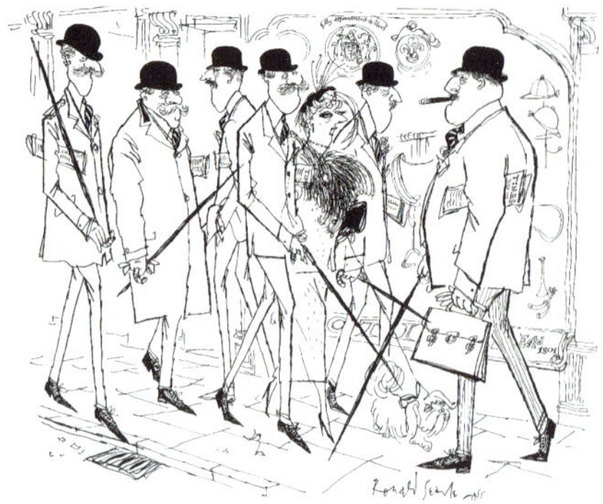

32 THE 'COKE'
signed and dated 1955
inscribed with title, publishing details and dated 1955 on reverse
pen and ink
12 x 15 inches
Illustrated: *Figaro*, Paris, 1955, 'England and the English' by Pierre Daninos

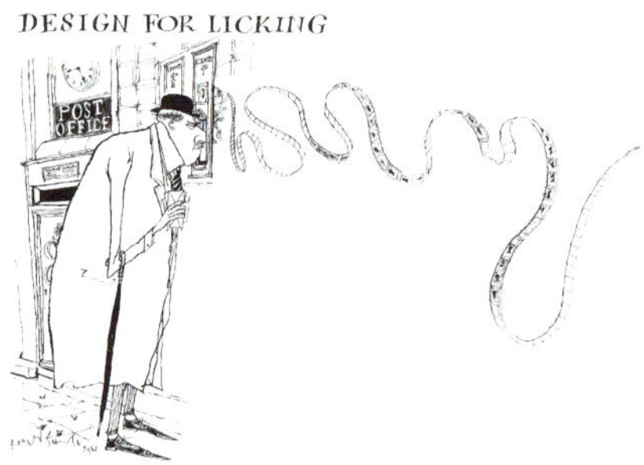

33 DESIGN FOR LICKING
signed and dated 1953
pen and ink
10 x 14 ½ inches

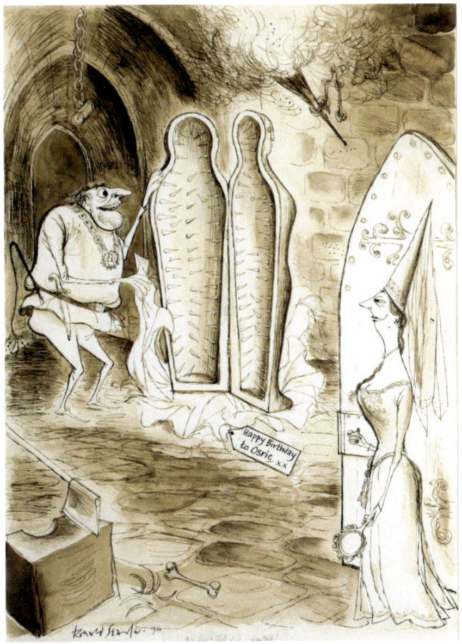

34 DARLING! – JUST WHAT I WANTED!
signed, inscribed with title and dated 1950
pen ink and monochrome watercolour
15 x 11 ¼ inches

Illustrated: *The Sketch*, 6 December 1950; Ronald Searle, *Back to the Slaughterhouse*, London: Macdonald, 1951, page 13; *Ronald Searle's Golden Oldies*, London: Pavilion, 1985, page 25

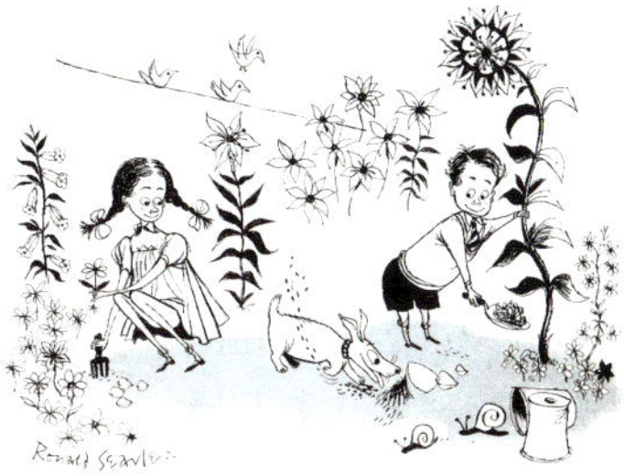

35 GARDENING
signed and inscribed with 'Herald Gardening'
pen ink with crayon
8 ½ x 11 ½ inches

Illustrated: *Daily Herald*, circa 1950

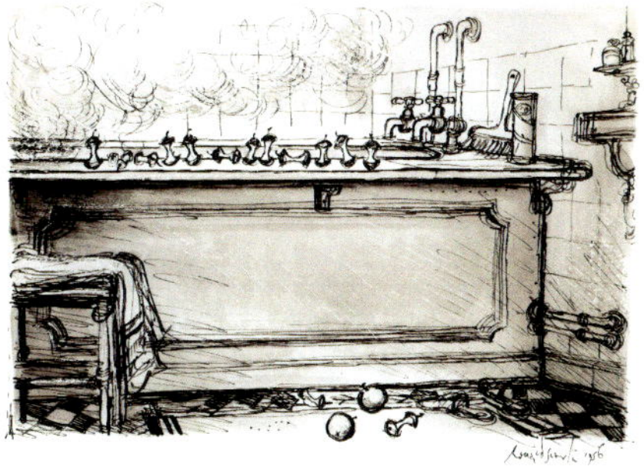

36 AGATHA CHRISTIE'S BATHTUB
signed and dated 1956
inscribed with title and 'Life Magazine' below mount
inscribed with title, publishing details and dated 1956 on reverse
pen ink and monochrome watercolour
7 ½ x 10 inches

Illustrated: *Life Magazine*, New York, 14 May 1956

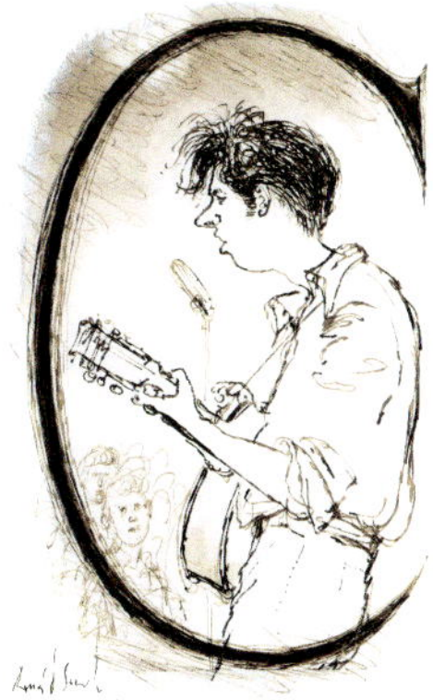

37 A HUBBUB OF MUSIC
signed
inscribed with 'A Night in a London Coffee House' below mount
pen and ink; 9 ¼ x 6 inches

Illustrated: Alex Atkinson and Ronald Searle, *The Big City*, London: Perpetua, 1958, page 63, 'Night in a London Coffee House'

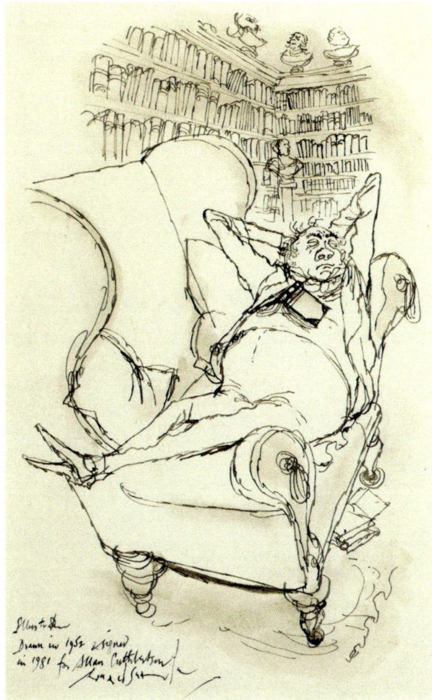

38 WHAT CALM AND PLEASANT SECLUSION THE LIBRARY PRESENTS
signed and inscribed 'Illustration drawn in 1952 & signed in 1981 for Allan Cuthbertson'
pen and ink
8 x 5 ½ inches

Drawn for but not illustrated in *Holiday*, November 1952

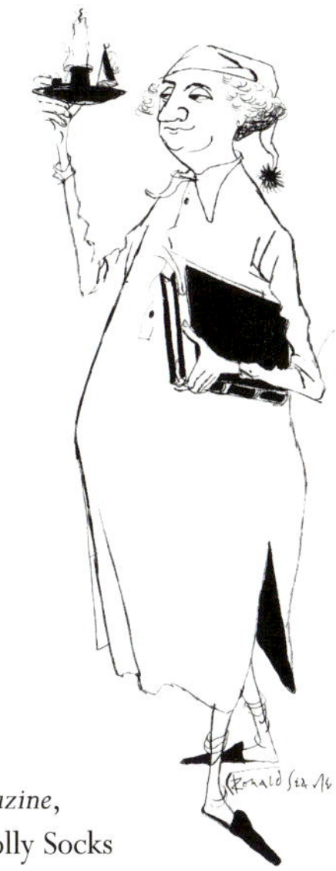

39 GEORGE WASHINGTON NEVER SLEPT IN THESE
printed signature and inscribed with title
pen and ink
14 x 8 ¾ inches

Illustrated: *New Yorker Magazine*, 1951, advertisement for Solly Socks

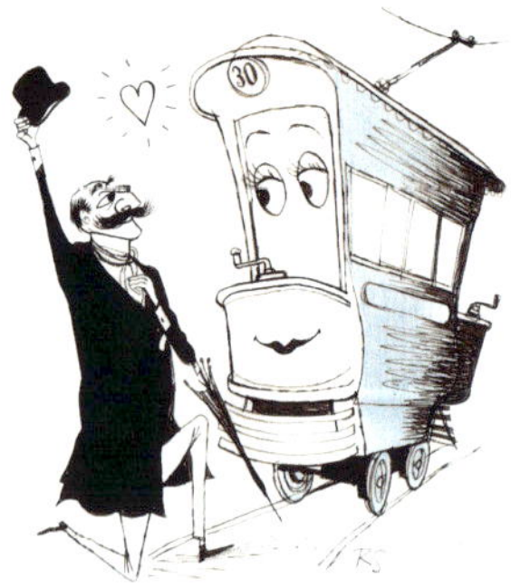

40 TRAM COURTING
signed with initials
inscribed 'Header Readers Letters' below mount
pen and ink with coloured pencil
8 ¼ x 7 ¾ inches
Illustrated: *Daily Herald*, circa 1950

Numbers 41-48 are all illustrated in Ronald Searle, *Merry England, Etc,* London: Perpetua, 1956.

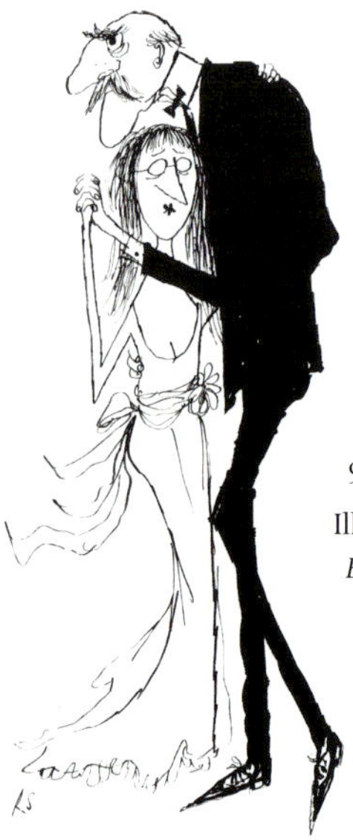

41 DANCING COUPLE
signed with initials
pen and ink
9 x 4 inches
Illustrated: *Merry England, Etc*, page 120

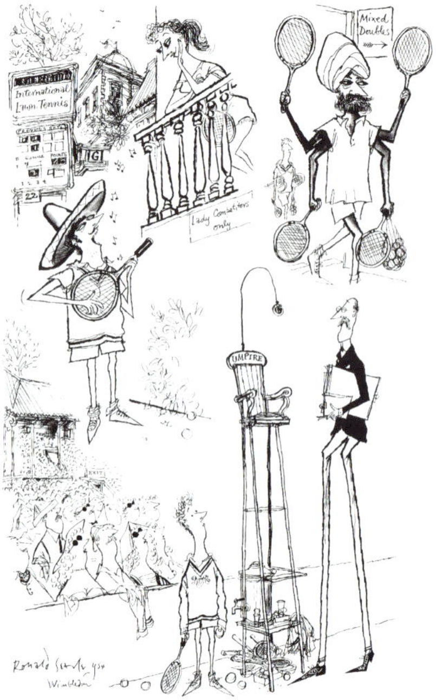

42 WIMBLEDON
signed, inscribed with title and dated 1954
pen ink and monochrome watercolour
20 ½ x 12 ½ inches
Illustrated: *News Chronicle*, 26 June 1954, 'Saturday Sketchbook';
Merry England, Etc, pages 60, 61 and 62;
The Penguin Ronald Searle, Harmondsworth: Penguin, 1960, unpaginated

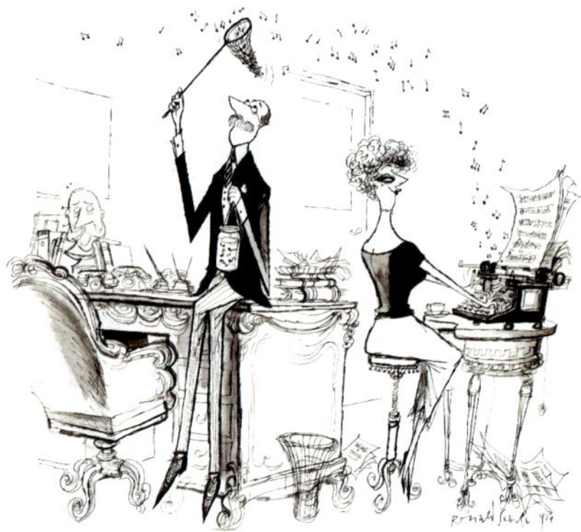

43 OFFICE DUO
signed and dated 1954
pen ink and monochrome watercolour
15 ½ x 18 ½ inches
Illustrated: *Punch*, 12 January 1955, page 97;
Merry England, Etc, page 19
Ronald Searle, *Pardong, M'sieur: Paris et autres*, Paris: Denoël, 1965

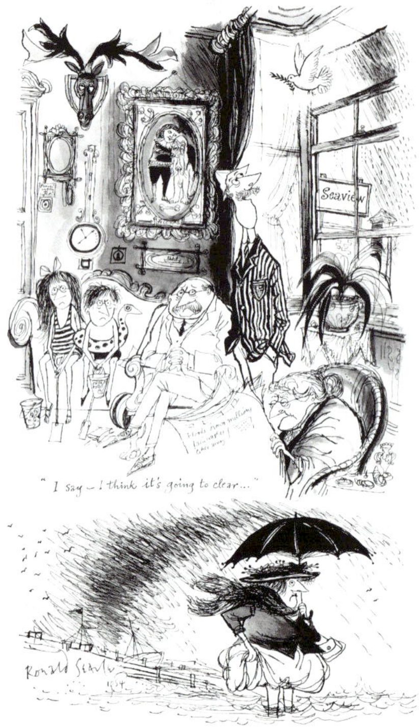

44 'I SAY – I THINK IT'S GOING TO CLEAR...'
SUMMER HOLIDAYS
signed, inscribed with title, 'News Chronicle' and dated 'Sat August 7th 1954'
pen ink and monochrome watercolour
20 x 12 ½ inches
Illustrated: *News Chronicle*, 7 August 1954;
Merry England, Etc, pages 73 and 74

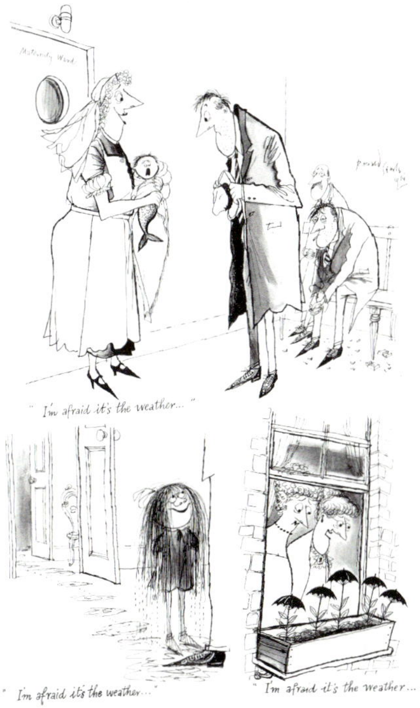

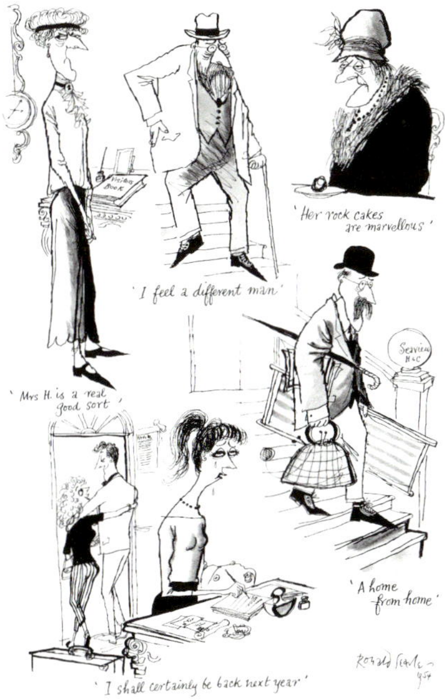

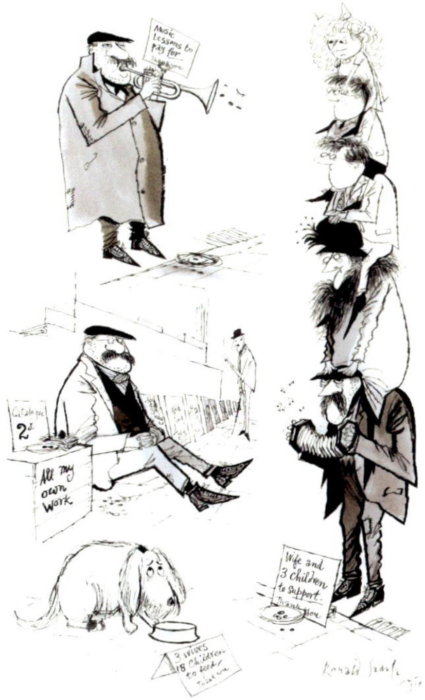

45 I'M AFRAID IT'S THE WEATHER
signed, inscribed with title and dated 1954
pen ink and monochrome watercolour
22 x 14 inches

Illustrated: *News Chronicle*, 14 August 1954, 'Saturday Sketchbook';
Merry England, Etc, pages 76 and 77;
The Penguin Ronald Searle, Harmondsworth: Penguin, 1960, unpaginated;
Ronald Searle's Golden Oldies, London: Pavilion, 1985, page 64

46 THE GUEST BOOK
signed and dated 1954
inscribed with title and dated 1954 on reverse
pen ink, watercolour and crayon
22 x 15 inches

Illustrated: *News Chronicle*, 23 August 1954;
Merry England, Etc, pages 69, 70, 71 and 72

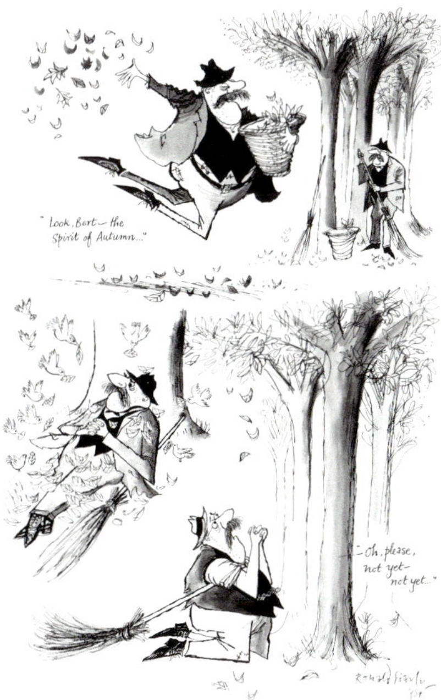

47 THE SPIRIT OF AUTUMN!
signed, inscribed with title and dated 1954
pen ink and monochrome watercolour
22 x 15 inches

Illustrated: *News Chronicle*, 25 September 1954;
Merry England, Etc, pages 96 and 97

48 STREET SCENES
signed and dated 1954
inscribed with title, publishing details and dated 1954 on reverse
pen and ink
22 x 14 ¾ inches

Illustrated: *News Chronicle*, 19 September 1954, page 4;
Merry England, Etc, pages 3, 7 and 82;
The Penguin Ronald Searle, Harmondsworth: Penguin 1960, unpaginated

Detail illustrated on back cover

Numbers 49-52 are all illustrated in Ronald Searle and Geoffrey Willans, *Down with Skool*, London: Max Parrish, 1953;
Ronald Searle and Geoffrey Willans, *The Compleet Molesworth*, London: Guild Publishing, 1985;
Geoffrey Willans and Ronald Searle, *Molesworth*, London: Penguin, 1999.

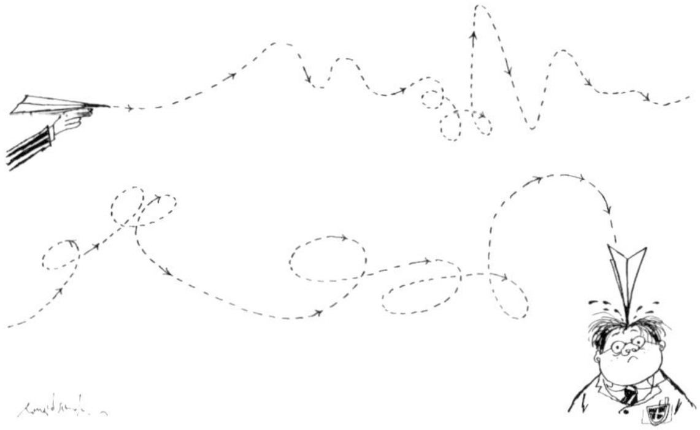

50 FLIGHT OF THE INK DART
signed, inscribed with title and 'Molesworth: Down with Skool pages 72/73 1953'
pen and ink
8 ¼ x 13 inches

Illustrated: *Down with Skool*, pages 72 and 73; *The Compleet Molesworth*, pages 72 and 73; *Molesworth*, pages 70 and 71

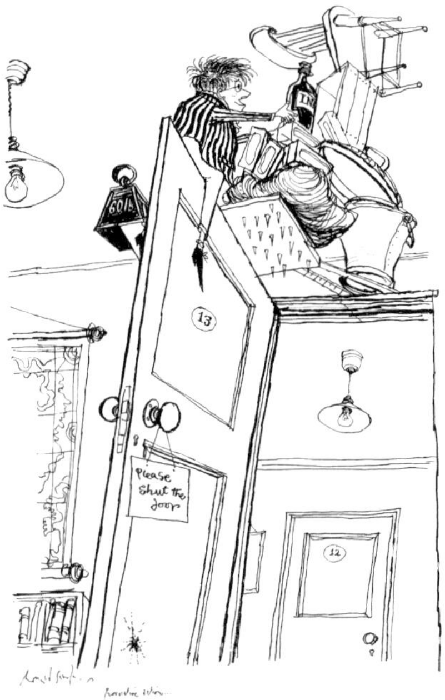

49 THAT'S ENUFF OF THAT FOR THE MOMENT. IN THE MEANTIME THIS SHOULD CONSTITUTE A PROVOCATIVE ACTION
signed and inscribed 'Provocative Action, Molesworth: Down with Skool. 1953 (page 72)'
pen and ink
13 x 9 ½ inches

Illustrated: *Down with Skool*, page 74; *The Compleet Molesworth*, page 74; *Molesworth*, page 72

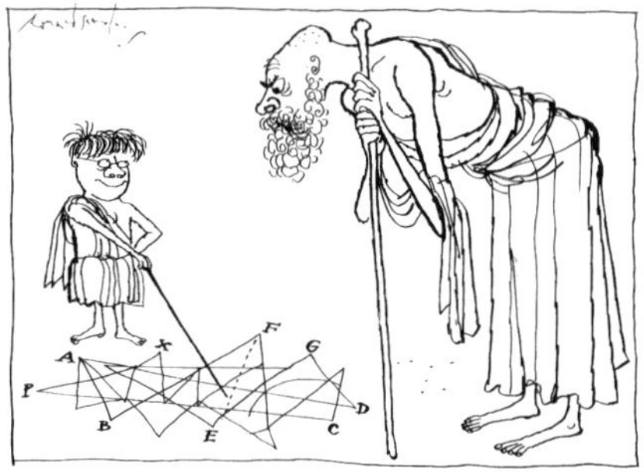

51 PYTHAGORAS PUZZLED BY ONE OF MY THEOREMS
signed
pen and ink
9 x 10 inches

Illustrated: *Down with Skool*, page 46; *The Compleet Molesworth*, page 46; *Molesworth*, page 44

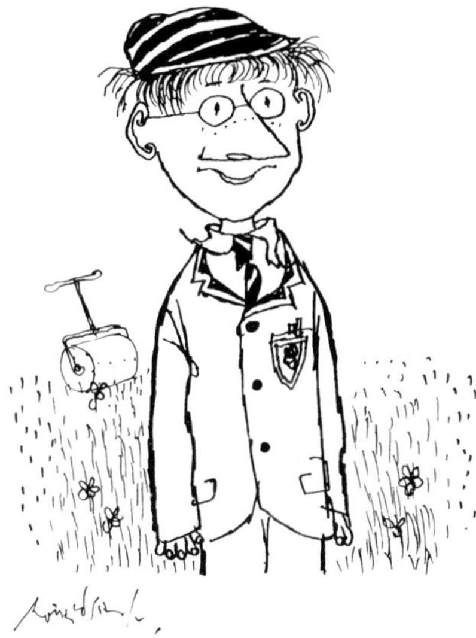

52 GOSH CHIZ THIS IS MOLESWORTH 2 MY BRO HE IS UTERLY WET AND A WEED IT PANES ME TO THINK I AM OF THE SAME BLUD
signed, inscribed 'Our camera club, Molesworth II by Molesworth I, Down with Skool page 12 1953'
pen and ink
9 x 7 ½ inches

Illustrated: *Down with Skool*, page 12; *The Compleet Molesworth*, page 12; *Molesworth*, page 10

Numbers 53-56 are all illustrated in Geoffrey Willans and Ronald Searle, *Whizz for Atomms*, London: Max Parrish, 1956. Numbers 55 and 56 are also illustrated in Ronald Searle and Geoffrey Willans, *The Compleet Molesworth*, London: Guild Publishing, 1985; Geoffrey Willans and Ronald Searle, *Molesworth*, London: Penguin, 1999.

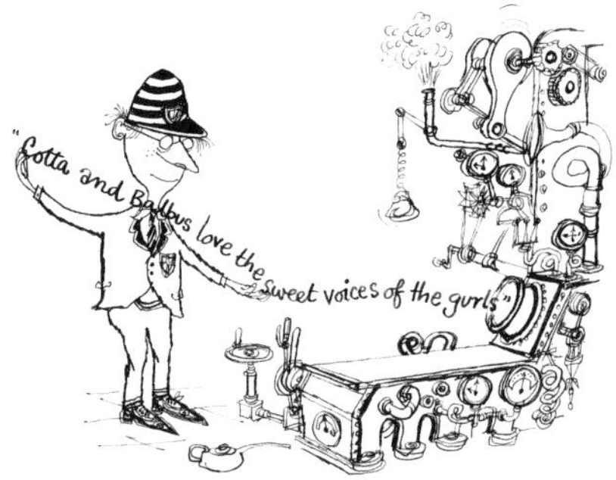

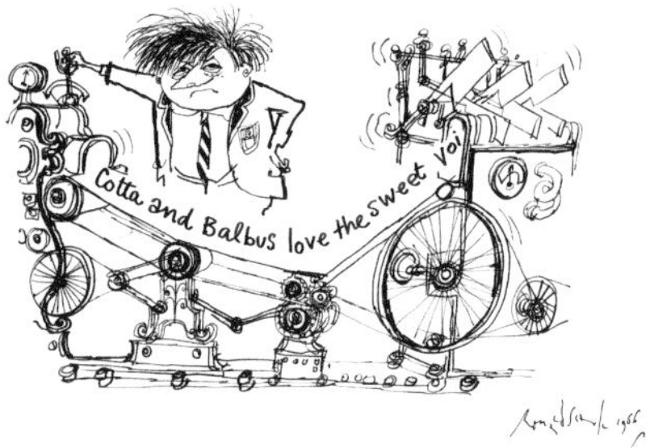

54 THE MOLESWORTH PRODUCTION LINE FOR LATIN SENTENCES
signed, inscribed with title and dated 1956
pen and ink
14 x 10 inches
Illustrated: *Whizz for Atomms*, page 102

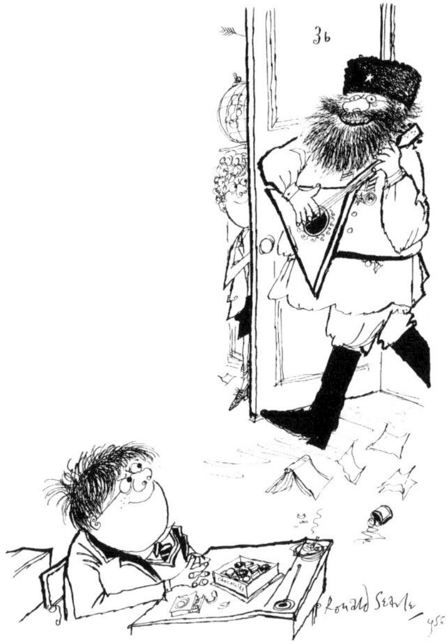

56 WE MITE GET A RUSIAN MASTER
signed and dated 1956
inscribed 'We must get a Rusian master at/St Custard's gosh golly you can/pikture it.../Whiz for Atomms [pp 60-61]' below mount
pen ink and blue crayon
12 x 9 ½ inches
Illustrated: *Whizz for Atomms*, pages 60 and 61; *The Compleet Molesworth*, pages 262 and 263; *Molesworth*, pages 264 and 265

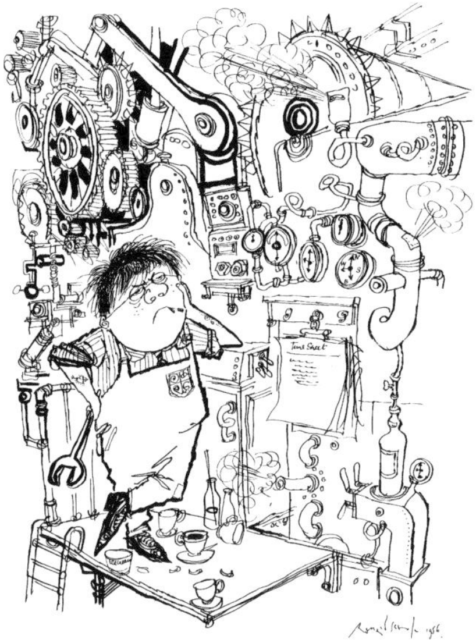

53 IT IS BY SUCH AN EXAMPLE AS I, LIKE THOSE OTHER BRAVE, CLEAR-EYED WORKERS IN THE DOCUMENTARY FILMS THAT BRITAIN WILL WIN ITS EXPORT BATTLE
signed, inscribed ' Molesworth: Brave, clear-eyed worker – as in documentary films..., Whizz for Atomms (page 99)' and dated 1956
pen and ink
13 ¼ x 10 ¼ inches
Illustrated: *Whizz for Atomms*, page 99

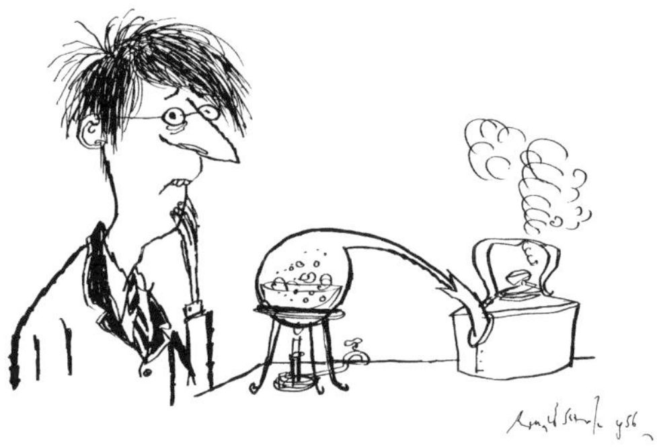

55 SHOULD HE MAKE HIS KNOLEDGE AVAILABLE TO EVERYONE?
signed, inscribed 'The Peason-Molesworth atommic pile: Whizz for Atomms (p. 41)' and dated 1956
pen ink and watercolour with crayon
14 x 12 ¼ inches
Illustrated: *Whizz for Atomms*, page 41; *The Compleet Molesworth*, page 243; *Molesworth*, page 245

Numbers 57 and 58 are both illustrated in Geoffrey Willans and Ronald Searle, *How to be Topp*, London: Max Parrish, 1954; Ronald Searle and Geoffrey Willans, *The Compleet Molesworth*, London: Guild Publishing, 1985; Geoffrey Willans and Ronald Searle, *Molesworth*, London: Penguin, 1999.

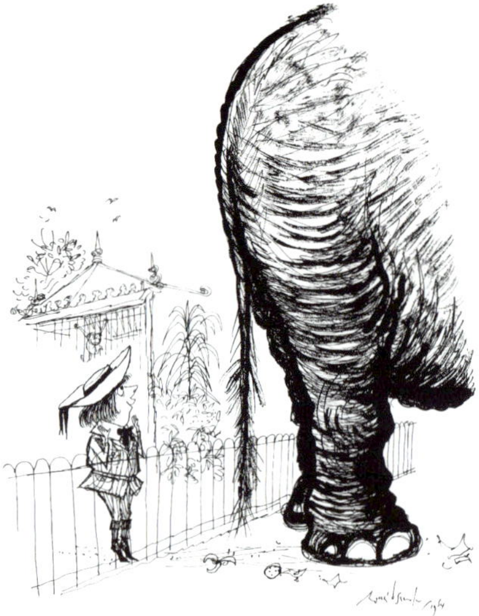

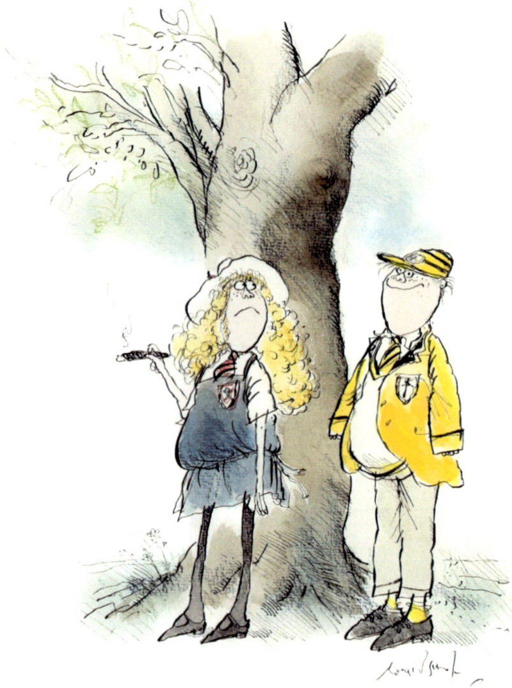

57 'HOW BIG THE ELEPHANTS ARE', OBSERVED ARMAND
signed, inscribed with title and dated 1954
pen and ink
14 x 10 ½ inches
Illustrated: *How to be Topp*, page 75; *The Compleet Molesworth*, page 175; *Molesworth*, page 175

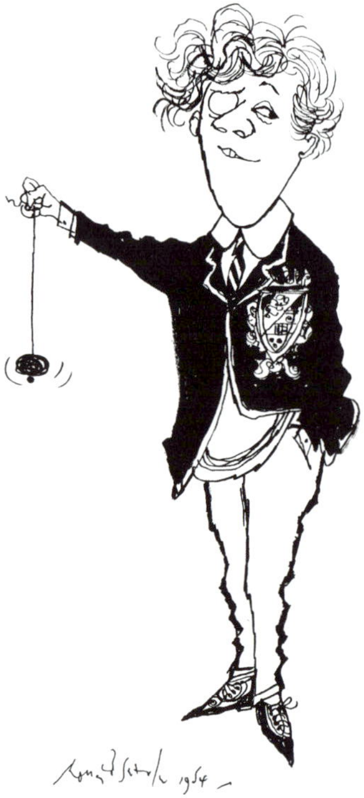

58 CAD WITH AN ANCESTRAL CONKER
signed, inscribed with title and 'Molesworth: How to be Topp (page 45)' and dated 1954
inscribed with title and 'They are inclined to cheat having baked them for 300 years in the ancestral oven...', publishing details and dated 1954 on reverse
pen and ink
11 ¼ x 8 ½ inches
Illustrated: *How to be Topp*, page 45; *The Compleet Molesworth*, page 145; *Molesworth*, page 145

59 ST TRINIANS MEETS ST CUSTARDS
signed and inscribed with title
pen ink, watercolour and coloured chalks
15 ½ x 11 ½ inches
Pencil drawings of the two figures below mount
Illustrated on front cover

60 RANK STARLET
signed, inscribed with title, 'To Phyllis Kirk with best wishes Ronald Searle artist' and dated 'Oct 1957'
pen and ink
9 ½ x 7 inches
Drawn on the front endpaper of Ronald Searle, *Merry England, Etc*, New York: Alfred A Knopf, 1957 (first American edition)

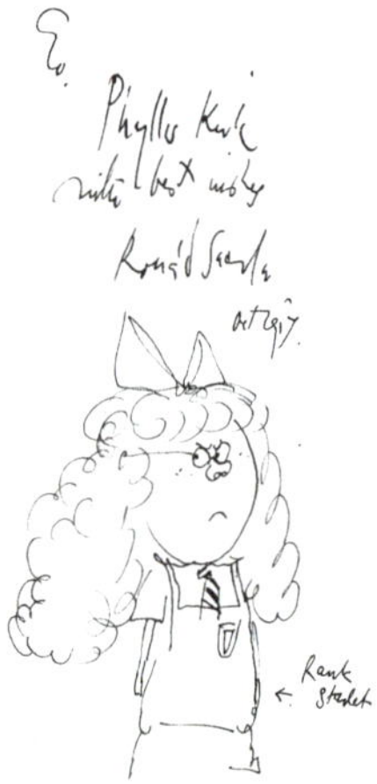

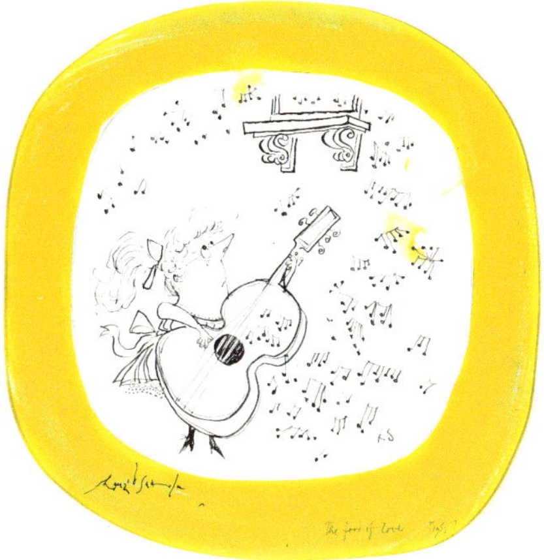

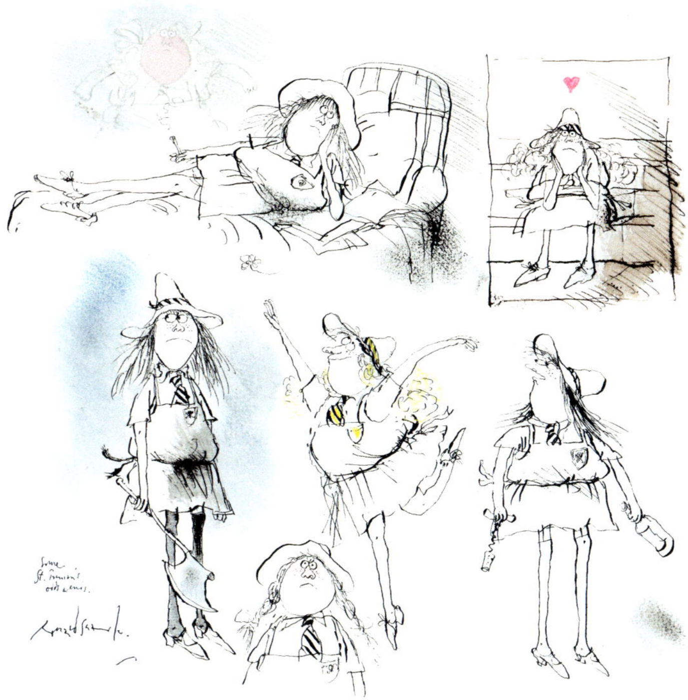

61 THE FOOD OF LOVE
signed, inscribed with title and dated 1957
inscribed 'The St Trinians Story: 1959 (page 76)'
and dated 1957 below mount
pen ink and bodycolour
8 x 9 inches

Illustrated: Ronald Searle, *The St Trinian's Story*, London: Perpetua, 1959, page 98; *Ronald Searle's Golden Oldies*, London: Pavilion, 1985, page 126 as 'Why can't he let down his hair, or something?'

Design for an ashtray by Nymolle Ceramics, Copenhagen

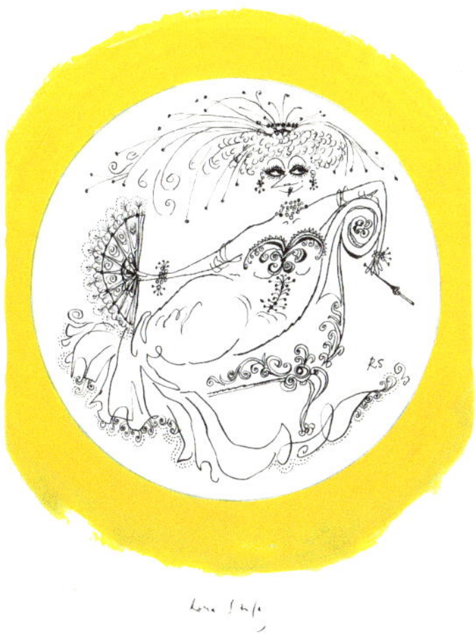

62 FEMME FATALE
signed, signed with initials, inscribed with title and dated 1957
pen ink and bodycolour
12 x 8 ¾ inches

Design for an plate by Nymolle Ceramics, Copenhagen

63 SOME ST TRINIANS ODDS AND ENDS
signed, inscribed with title and dated '1950?'
inscribed 'St Trinians notes' and dated '1950ish' on reverse
pen ink and watercolour with crayon
13 ¾ x 14 inches

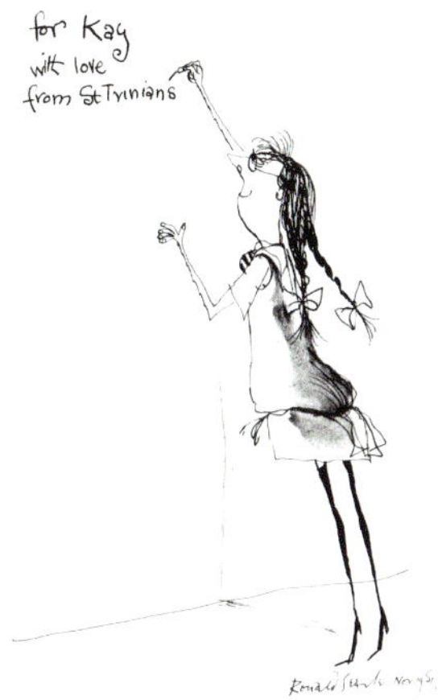

64 ST TRINIANS GRAFFITI
signed, inscribed 'For Kay with love from St Trinians' and dated 'Nov 1951'
pen and ink
7 ¾ x 5 inches

Drawn on the front endpaper of Ronald Searle, *Back to the Slaughterhouse*, London: Macdonald, 1951

Numbers 65-68 are all illustrated in Kaye Webb and Ronald Searle, *Refugees, 1960*, Harmondsworth: Penguin, 1960. Relevant excerpts are given below

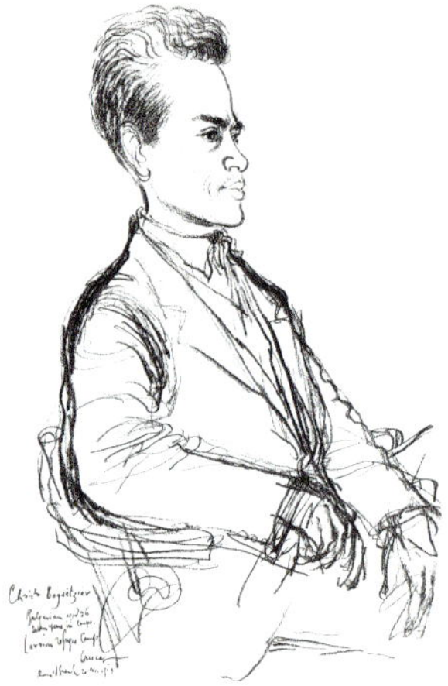

65 CHRISTO BOGAITZIEV, BULGARIAN AGED 26. SEVEN YEARS IN CAMPS. LAVRION REFUGEE CAMP, GREECE.
signed, inscribed with title and dated '20 Nov 1959'
pen ink and pencil
15 x 11 inches
Illustrated: *Punch*, 30 December 1959, page 666; *Refugees, 1960*, page 46

'Christo Bogaitziev escaped from Bulgaria to Greece when he was nineteen. He is now twenty-six. He has twice been accepted for emigration overseas, but both times excitement affected his reason, and so he lost his visa. Although he has been stable for more than a year, he no longer hopes for a third chance and would be content to be allowed to work and use his languages. In his seven years of waiting he taught himself Italian, Russian, French, Greek, and English. Now he wants only a room of his own, books to read, and a positive future. "What I can't endure is this in-between state".'

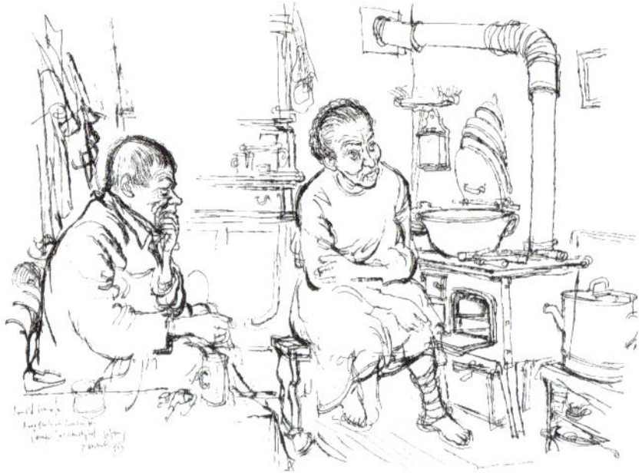

66 ANNA BARTH AND LEONARD HESS. CAMP LASCHENSKY-HOF, SALZBURG
signed, inscribed with title and dated '7 November 1959'
pen and ink
15 x 21 ¼ inches
Illustrated: *Punch*, 30 December 1959, page 657; *Refugees, 1960*, page 20

'Anna Barth, the woman in this picture, is forty-five years old. She comes from Yugoslavia. In the last war she and her crippled husband were told to hand over German soldiers who were billeted with them. They refused, and so the partisans murdered her husband. At war's end she and her four children were taken to a prison labour camp. Her young son was beaten to death by camp guards and two of her daughters died of starvation. She then had twelve of her teeth pulled out and gave the gold fillings to pay for bread for the last child. "But she was too weak. She died holding the loaf in her arms!".'

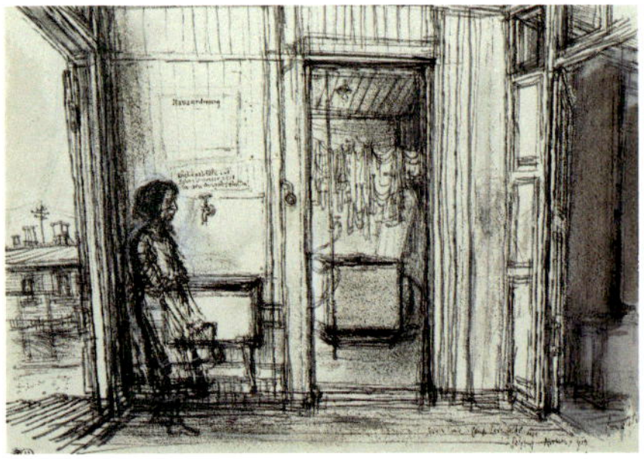

67 WASH HOUSE, CAMP LEXENFELDSTRASSE, SALZBURG
signed, inscribed with title and dated '7 November 1959'
pen ink and monochrome watercolour on tinted paper; 15 ½ x 21 ½ inches
Illustrated: *Refugees, 1960*, page 18 and back cover

'A washroom in camp Lexenfeldstrasse, Salzburg, is typical of those in every official refugee camp. At the end of a long dismal corridor an unpainted gloomy room with basins of either stone of galvanized metal. It was constantly in use, for washing or ironing seemed almost the only occupation for women refugees. Although this was, in a sense, the only communal room in the camp, there was very little conversation or friendliness between the women who used it. They had lived together so long, and so little had happened to them, that there was nothing left to say. They had no homes to be proud of, no work to grumble about, and no news to exchange.'

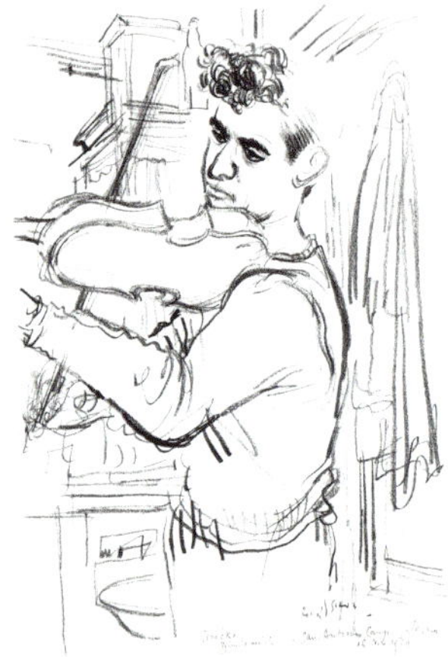

68 ISRECKO DIMITRIYEVICH, SAN ANTONIO CAMP, SALERNO
signed, inscribed with title and dated '16 Nov 1959'
pencil
18 ½ x 12 ½ inches
Illustrated: *Refugees, 1960*, page 35

'Isrecko Dimitriyevich has escaped twice. The first time, in 1957, he was sent back as under age and put in prison. When he was released he escaped again and joined his mother and brother in San Antonio camp, Naples. Isrecko's father was a musician killed in the war. He himself works tirelessly, believing that one day he will get to the United States to continue his training.'

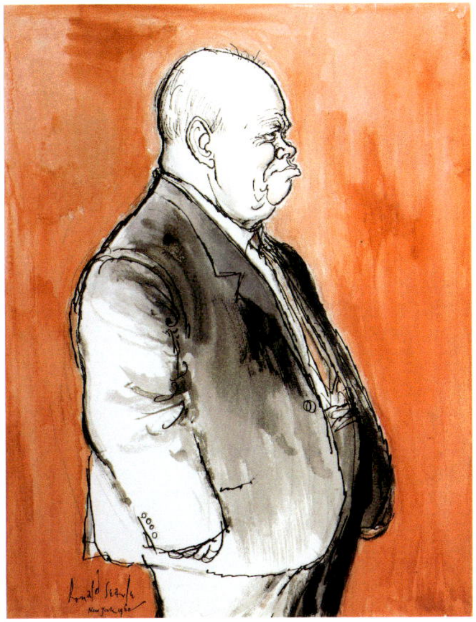

69 NIKITA KHRUSHCHEV
signed, inscribed 'New York' and dated 1960
pen ink and watercolour; 15 ¾ x 12 inches
Illustrated: *Holiday*, New York, February 1961, page 56, 'Khrushchev' by Maurice Edelman; *Searle in the Sixties*, Harmondsworth: Penguin, 1964, unpaginated;
Illustrated: Russell Davies, *Ronald Searle*, London: Sinclair-Stevenson, 1990, page 134

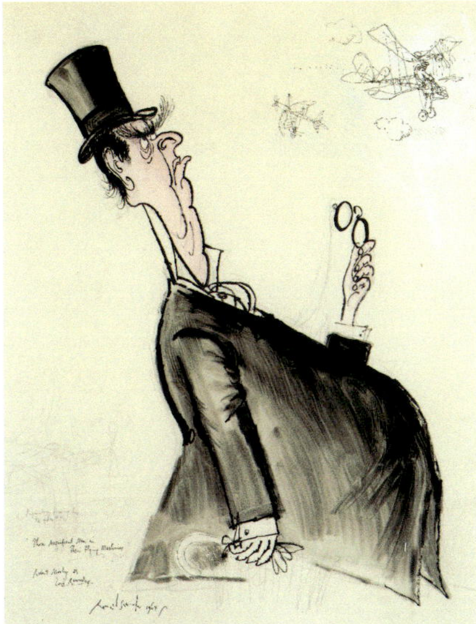

70 ROBERT MORLEY AS LORD RAWNSLEY
signed, inscribed with title, 'Preparatory drawings for the film titles "Those Magnificent Men in Their Flying Machines" [1965]' and dated 1964
pen ink, watercolour and pencil
20 ½ x 15 ¾ inches
Preparatory drawing for the film titles of *Those Magnificent Men in Their Flying Machines*, 1964. Similar to the illustration in Ronald Searle, Bill Richardson and Allen Andrews, *Those Magnificent Men in Their Flying Machines*, London: Dennis Dobson, 1965, page 40

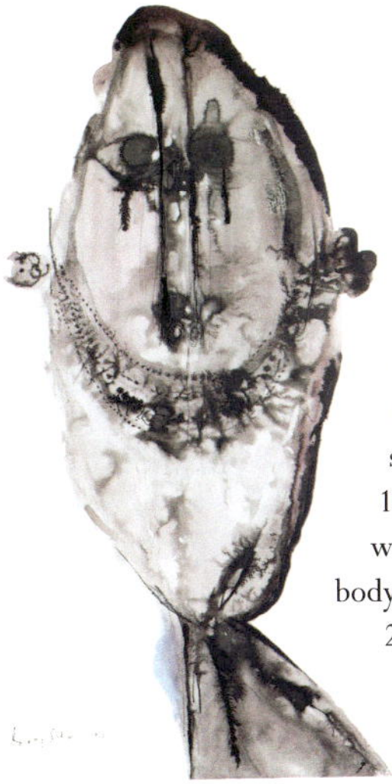

71
HEAD
signed and dated 1963
watercolour, bodycolour and ink
29 x 20 inches

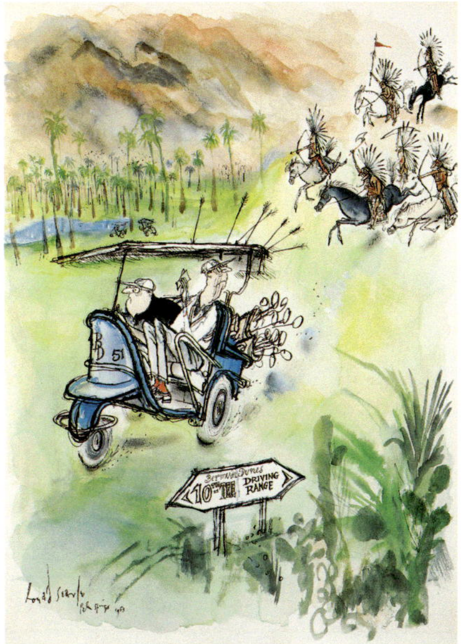

72 BERMUDA DUNES GOLF COURSE, PALM SPRINGS
signed, inscribed 'Palm Springs' and dated 1963
inscribed with title and publishing details on reverse
pen ink and watercolour; 19 x 14 inches
Illustrated: *Holiday*, New York, February 1965

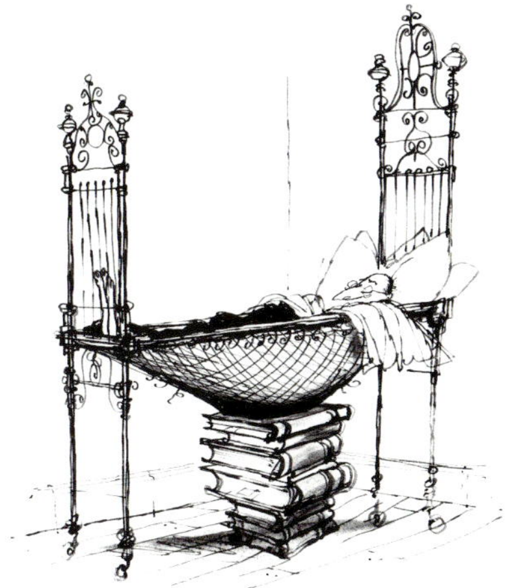

73 BEDTIME READING
pen and ink
11 x 15 ½ inches
Illustrated: Ronald Searle, *Which Way Did He Go?*, London: Perpetua, 1961, page 30, 'This Precious Stone Set in the Silver Sea'; *Ronald Searle's Golden Oldies*, London: Pavilion, 1985, page 40

Numbers 74 – 83 are all from a series in *Punch* entitled 'Searle's-eye View'

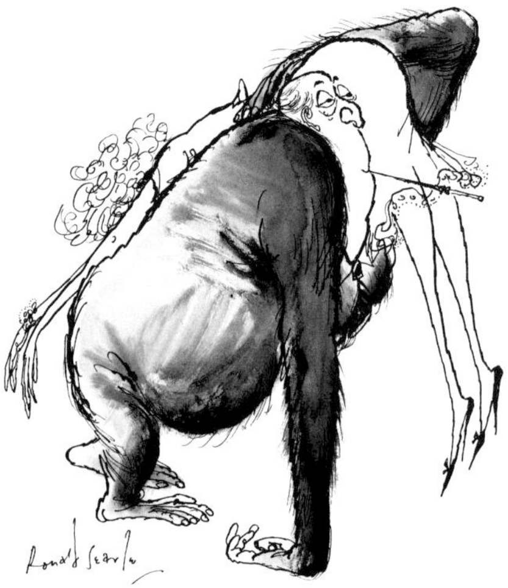

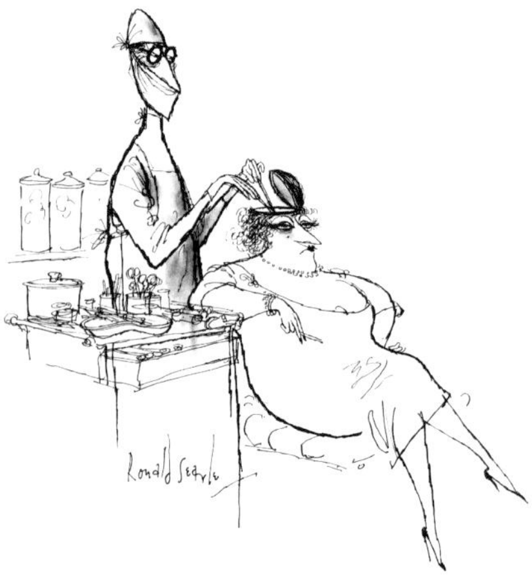

75 NO 13: ANGUS WILSON
signed, inscribed 'Imaginary Portraits 13 Angus Wilson' and 'Punch' and dated '21 Feb 1962'
pen ink and monochrome watercolour
13 ½ x 13 ¾ inches
Illustrated: *Punch*, 21 February 1962, page 334

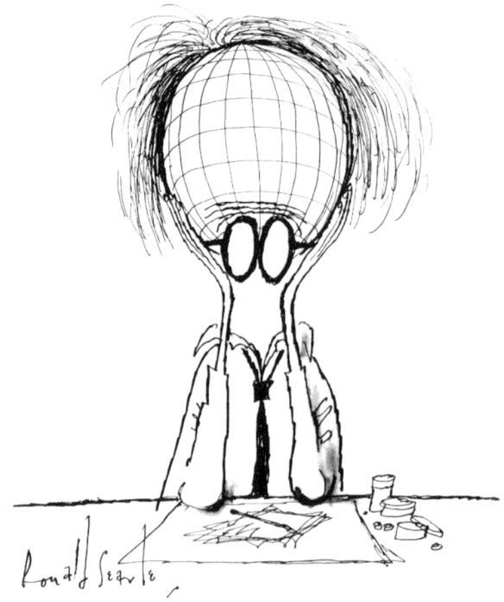

76 NO 18: ALDOUS HUXLEY
signed, inscribed 'Imaginary Portraits 18 Aldous Huxley' and 'Punch' and dated '28 March 1962'
pen and ink
15 ¼ x 12 ½ inches
Illustrated: *Punch*, 28 March 1962, page 514

74 NO 33: IAN FLEMING
signed, inscribed 'Imaginary Portraits 33 Ian Fleming' and dated 1962
pen ink and monochrome watercolour
16 ½ x 15 inches
Illustrated: *Punch*, 18 July 1962, page 104; *Searle in the Sixties*, Harmondsworth: Penguin, 1964, unpaginated

77 NO 39: C NORTHCOTE PARKINSON
signed, inscribed 'Imaginary Portraits 39 C Northcote Parkinson' and 'Punch' and dated '29 August 1962'
pen ink and monochrome watercolour
15 ½ x 13 inches
Illustrated: *Punch*, 29 August 1962, page 320

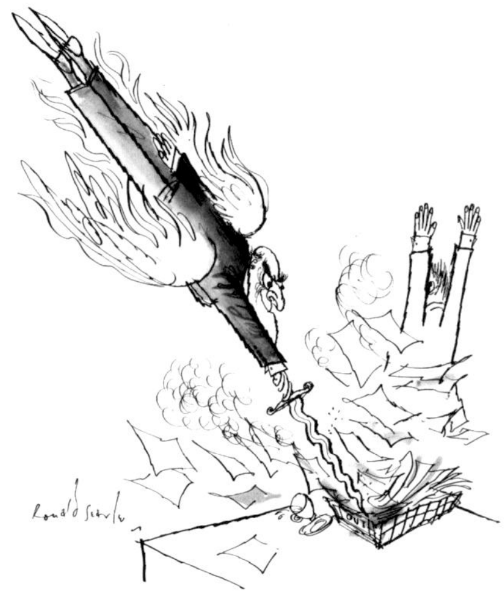

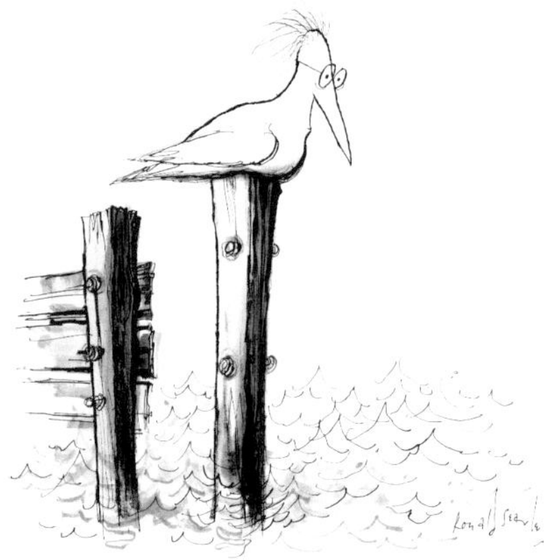

78 NO 25: BENJAMIN BRITTEN
signed, inscribed 'Imaginary Portraits 30 Benjamin Britten' and 'Punch' and dated '23 May 1962'
pen ink and monochrome watercolour
14 x 13 inches
Illustrated: *Punch*, 23 May 1962, page 806; *Searle in the Sixties*, Harmondsworth: Penguin, 1964, unpaginated

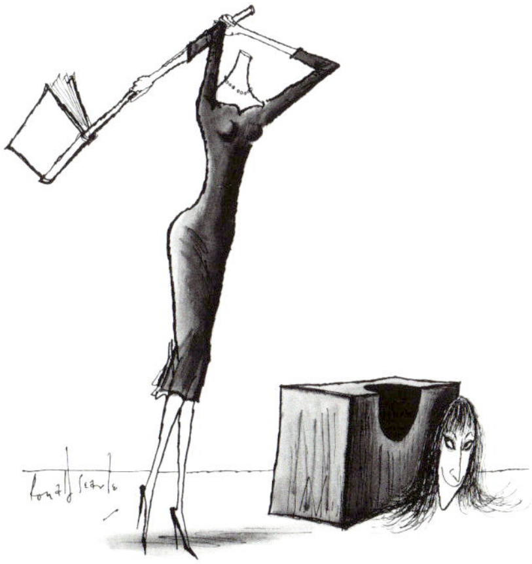

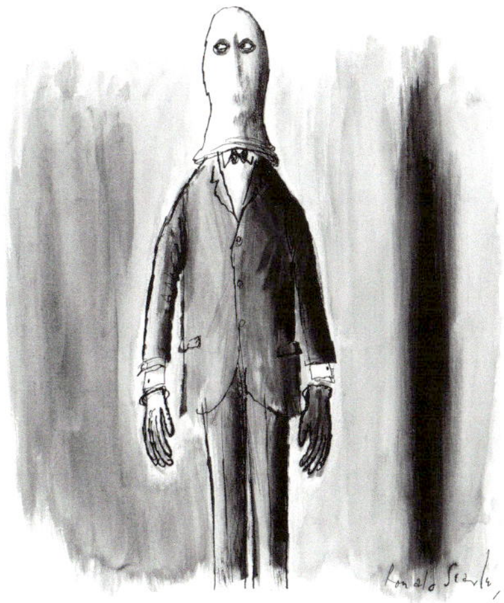

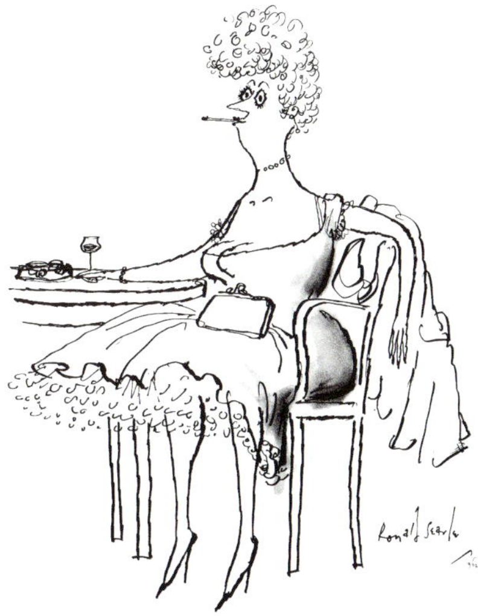

81 NO 27: ALFRED HITCHCOCK
signed, inscribed 'Imaginary Portraits 29 Alfred Hitchcock' and dated 1962
pen ink and monochrome watercolour
15 ½ x 13 inches
Illustrated: *Punch*, 6 June 1962, page 882

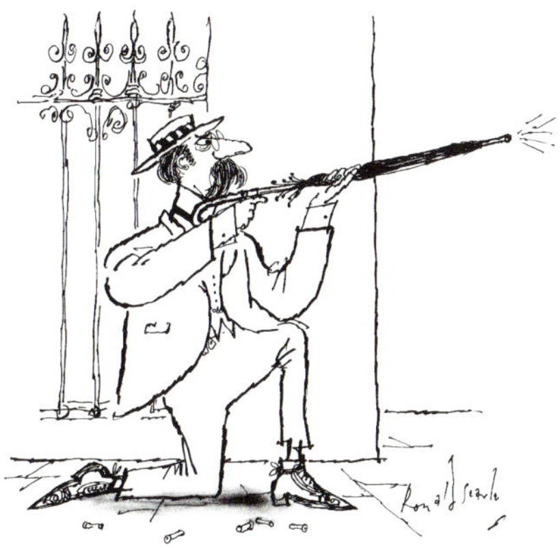

79 NO 17: IRIS MURDOCH
signed, inscribed 'Imaginary Portraits 17 Iris Murdoch' and dated '21 March 1962'
pen ink and monochrome watercolour
16 x 16 inches
Illustrated: *Punch*, 21 March 1962, page 478; *Searle in the Sixties*, Harmondsworth: Penguin, 1964, unpaginated

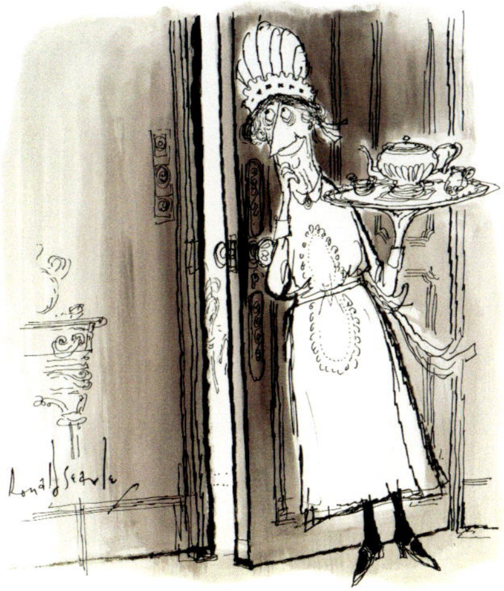

80 NO 29: JOHN BETJEMAN
signed, inscribed 'Imaginary Portraits John Betjeman' and 'Punch' and dated '20th June 1962'
pen and ink
11 x 12 inches
Illustrated: *Punch*, 20 June 1962, page 954; *Searle in the Sixties*, Harmondsworth: Penguin, 1964, unpaginated

82 NO 36: SHELAGH DELANEY
signed, inscribed 'Imaginary Portraits Shelagh Delaney' and dated 1962
pen and ink
16 ½ x 13 inches
Illustrated: *Punch*, 8 August 1962, page 212

83 NO 15: IVY COMPTON-BURNETT
signed
pen ink and monochrome watercolour
15 ¾ x 14 ½ inches
Illustrated: *Punch*, 7 March 1962, page 406; *Searle in the Sixties*, Harmondsworth: Penguin, 1964, unpaginated

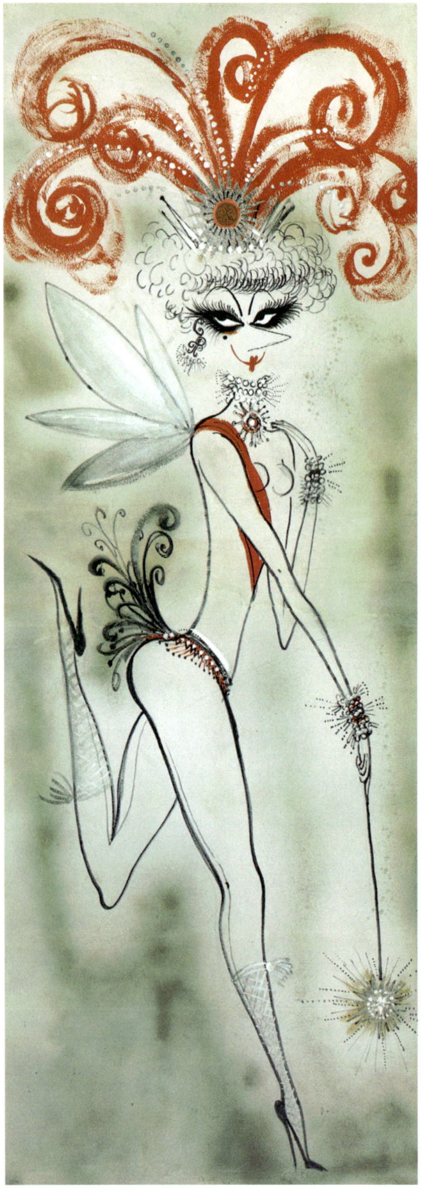

84 NEW YEAR'S FAIRY
pen ink, bodycolour and collage
53 ½ x 20 ¾ inches

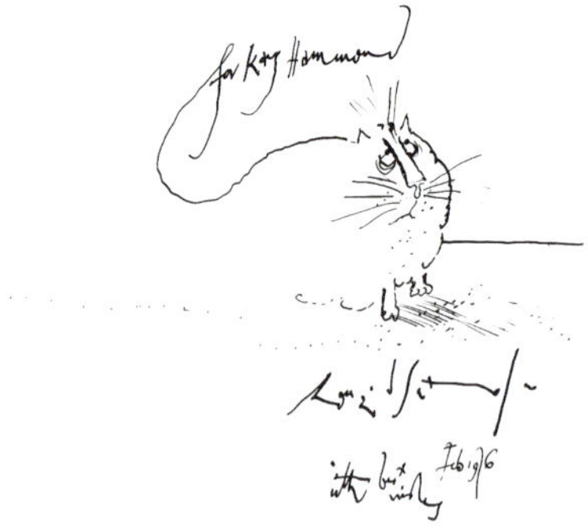

85 MORE CATS
signed, inscribed 'For Kay Hammond' and 'with best wishes' and dated 'Feb 1976'
pen and ink
4 x 3 ¾ inches

Drawn on the front endpaper of Ronald Searle, *More Cats*, London: Dennis Dobson, 1975

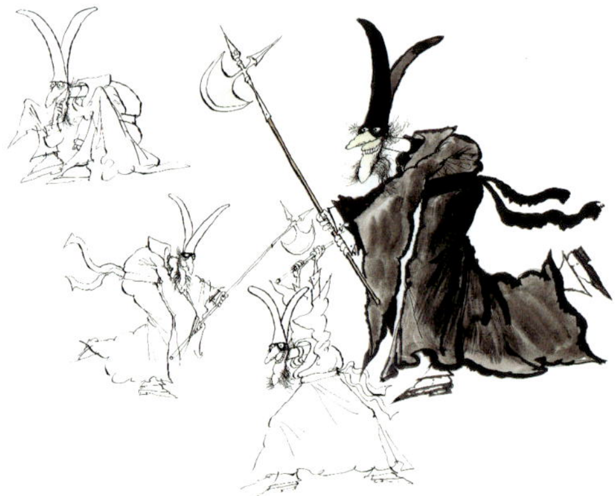

86 THE SORCERER AS EXECUTIONER
inscribed with title
Ronald Searle studio stamp below mount
pen ink and monochrome watercolour
17 x 22 inches

Drawing for *Dick Deadeye*, an animated film based on the Savoy operas of Gilbert & Sullivan, produced by Bill Melendez and Leo Rost in 1975; and for the book Ronald Searle and Gilbert & Sullivan, *Dick Deadeye*, London: Jonathan Cape, 1975. Drawn for the final episode on the desert island which turns out to be Utopia.

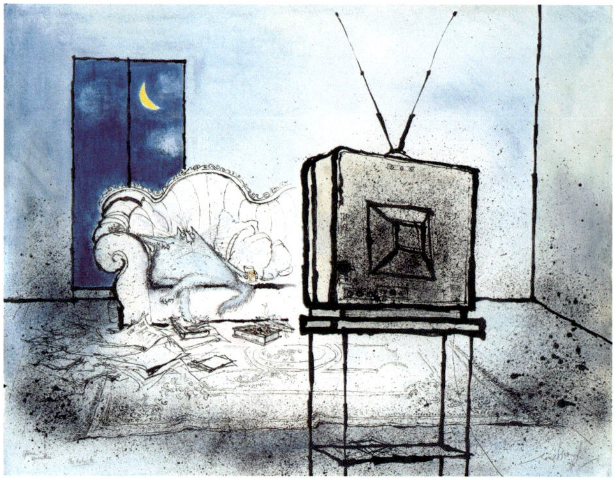

87 THE BABYSITTER
signed, inscribed with title, 'epreuve aquarellee' and dated 1976
lithograph with pencil, watercolour and coloured chalks
20 x 26 inches

Published by Ronald Searle and Atelier Michel Cassé, Paris, 1976

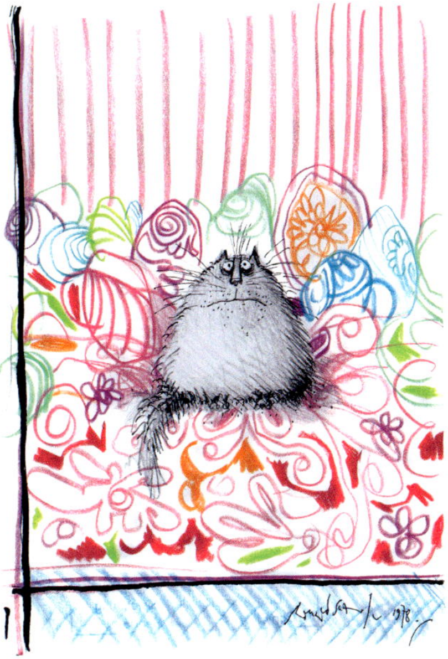

88 SITTING PRETTY
signed and dated 1978
inscribed with title, publishing details and dated 1978 on reverse
pen ink, pencil and crayon; 8 ¼ x 6 inches
Preliminary drawing for the *New Yorker*, 15 January 1979, cover

Illustrated on title page

89 FAMILY PHOTO
signed, inscribed 'For Simon Bond with best wishes Ronald Searle' and dated 1983
pen ink, pencil and watercolour
8 x 5 ½ inches
Similar to *Ronald Searle's Big Fat Cat Book*, London: Macmillan, 1982, frontispiece

90 GUILIO CESARE IN EGITTO
signed, inscribed with title and dated 1988
inscribed with title and 'For the Metropolitan Opera, New York' on reverse
pen and ink
13 ½ x 13 inches
Produced for the Metropolitan Opera, New York

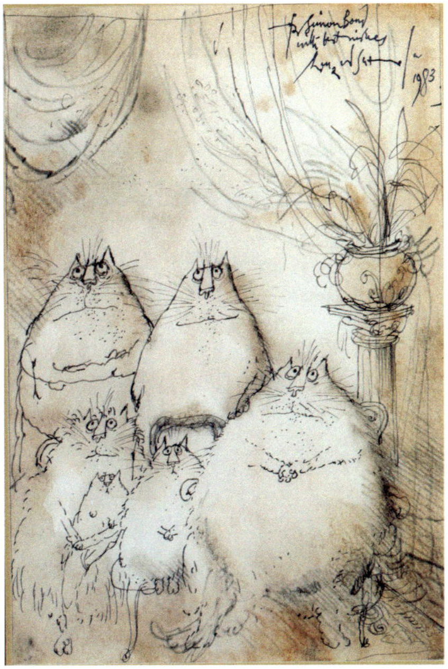

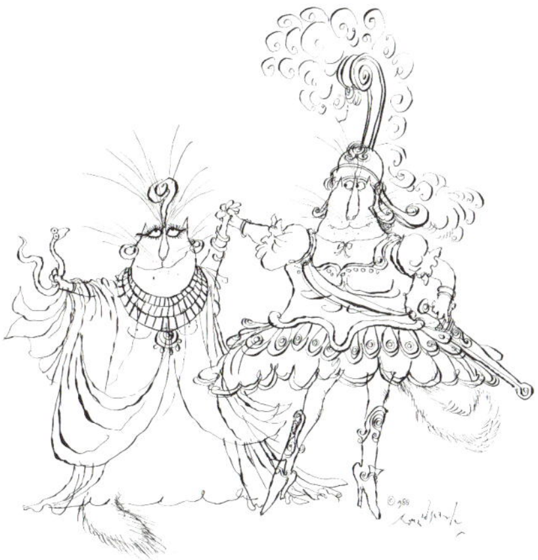

91 CRACKERS
signed
inscribed with title, publishing details and dated 1982 on reverse of mount board
watercolour, pen ink and crayon
12 x 9 ¼ inches
Design for a Christmas card for Camden Graphics, London, 1982

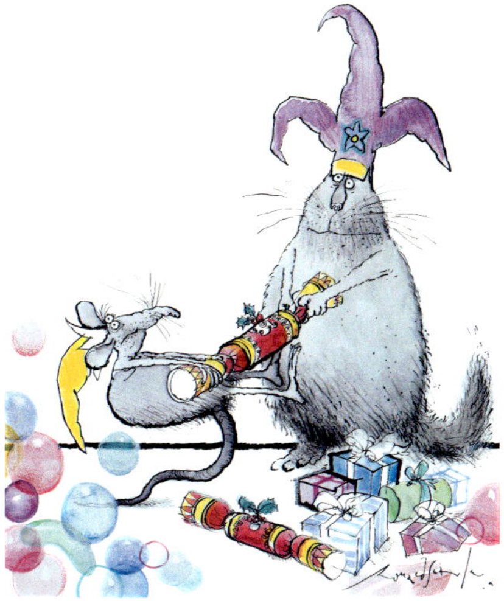

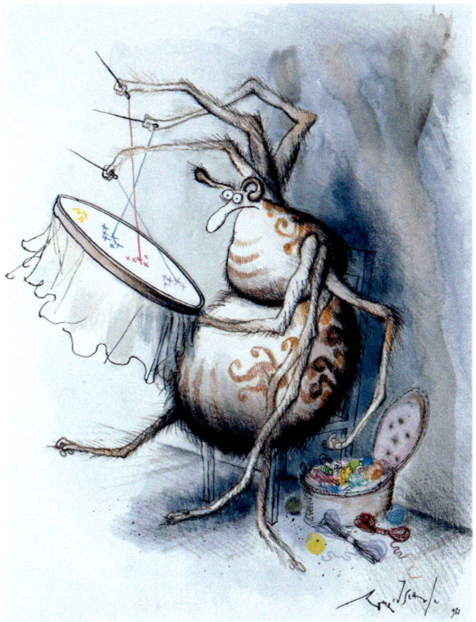

92 CONFUSED ARACHNID EMBROIDERING A FLY TRAP
signed and dated 1983
inscribed with title, publishing details and dated 1983 on reverse
pen ink and watercolour with crayon and bodycolour; 14 x 11 ¼ inches
Illustrated: *Animal Kingdom*, New York, April 1984

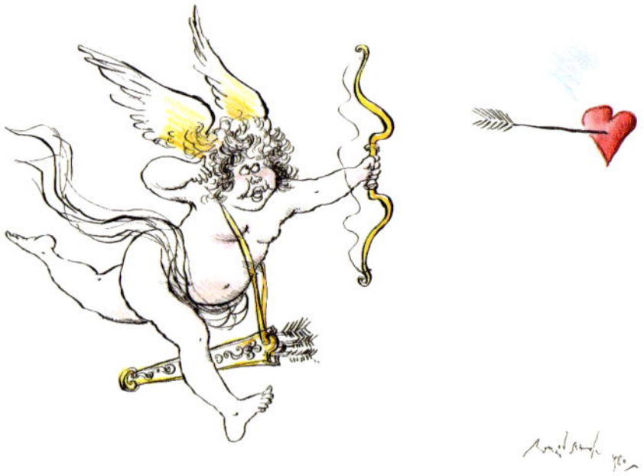

93 FOR A VALENTINE
signed, inscribed with title and dated 1980
pen ink and watercolour with crayon
13 x 16 ¾ inches

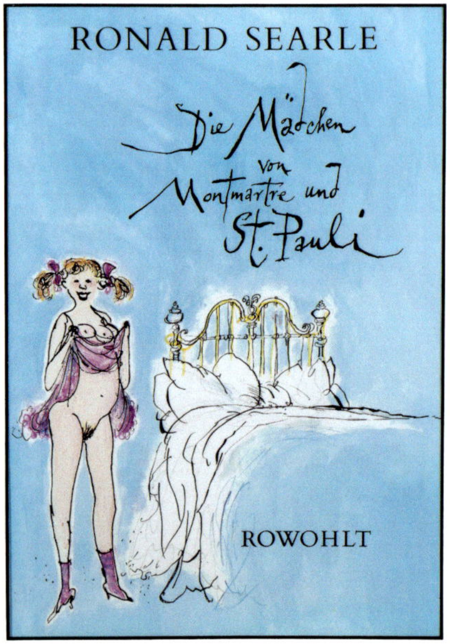

94 DIE MADCHEN VON MONTMARTRE UND ST PAULI
pen ink, watercolour and crayon, with overlay
11 x 8 inches
Illustrated: Ronald Searle, *Die Madchen von Montmartre und St Pauli*, Reinbek: Rowohlt, 1980, dustjacket

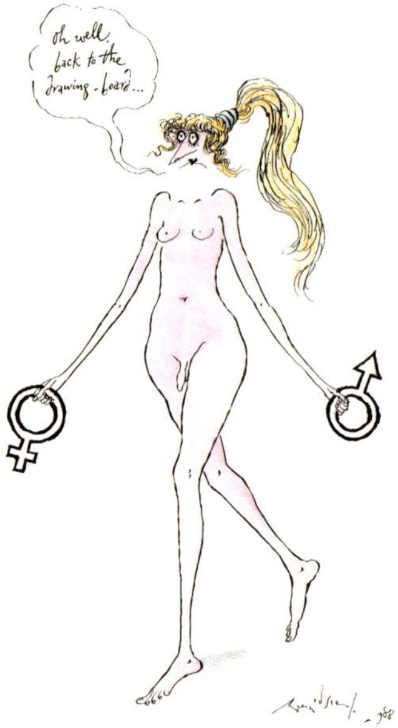

95 HERMAPHRODITE – HIMAPHRODITE
signed and dated 1988
pen ink and watercolour with crayon
14 ¾ x 10 inches
Pen and ink drawing of a kneeling woman on reverse
Similar to the illustration in *Ronald Searle's Non-Sexist Dictionary*, London: Souvenir Press, 1988, unpaginated

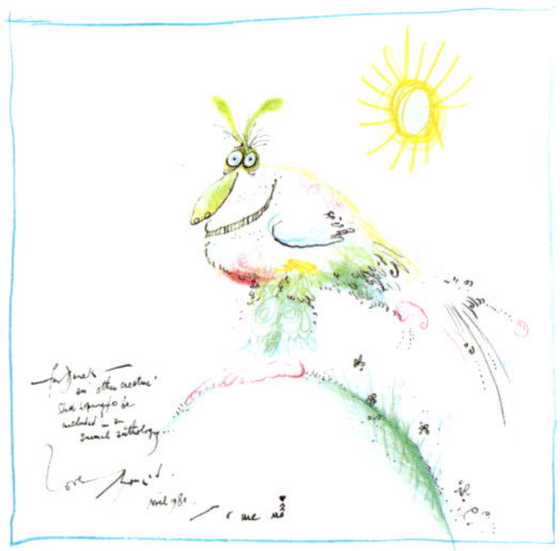

96 AN 'OTHER CREATURE'
signed, inscribed ' – For Derek – an 'other creature' still hoping to be included in an animal anthology...' and 'love Ronald' and dated 'Noel 1980'
pen ink and coloured crayon
8 ¼ x 9 inches

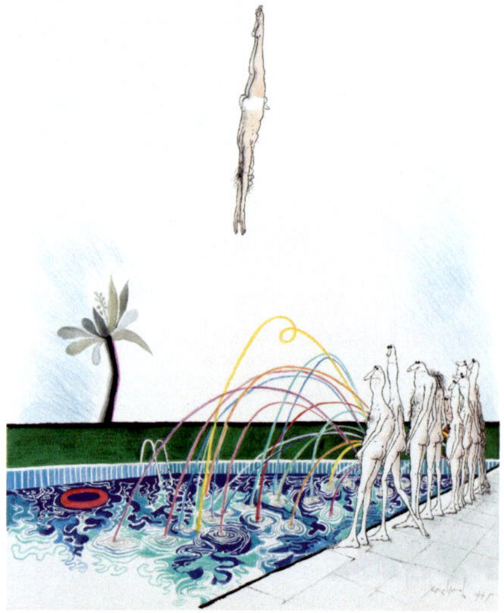

97 A BIGGER SLASH, HOMAGE A DAVID HOCKNEY
signed, inscribed with title and 'b&w water-colour maquette' and dated 1984
lithograph with crayon and watercolour
25 ½ x 20 inches
Published by Ronald Searle and Atelier Michel Cassé, Paris, 1984
Illustrated: Russell Davies, *Ronald Searle*, London: Sinclair-Stevenson, 1990, between pages 176 and 177

Numbers 99, 100, 102 and 103 are all illustrations for Lloyds Bank brochures.

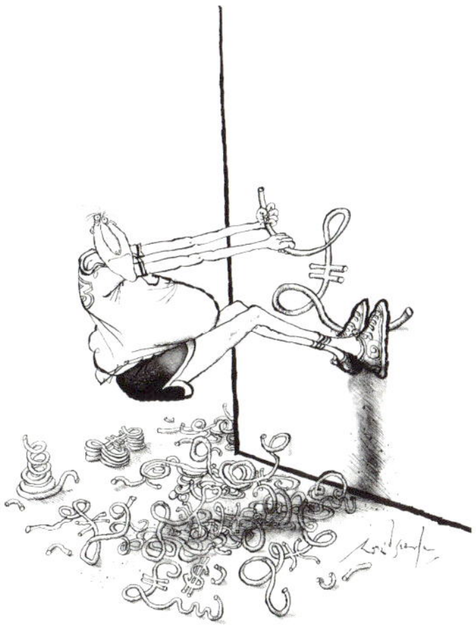

98 WHITHER THE POUND?
signed, inscribed with title and dated 1983
pen ink, pencil and monochrome watercolour
16 ½ x 12 inches

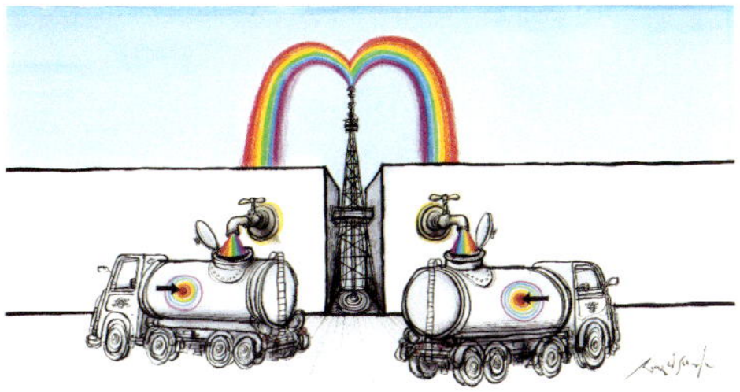

99 ANOTHER DAY, ANOTHER DOLLAR
signed and inscribed with title
dated 1981 on reverse
pen ink and watercolour with bodycolour
11 x 18 ½ inches

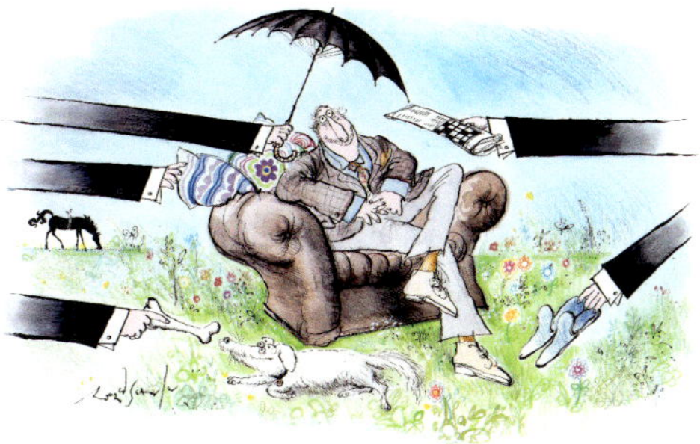

100 GLORIOUS RETIREMENT
signed, inscribed with title and dated 1981
watercolour, pen ink and crayon
11 ¾ x 18 ½ inches

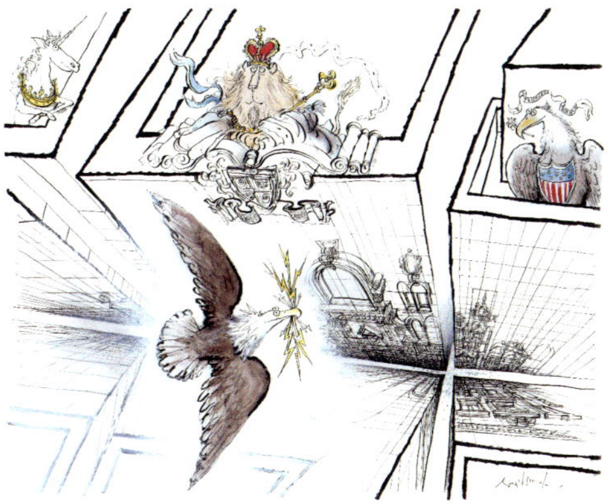

101 A CLASH OF SYMBOLS
signed
Ronald Searle studio stamp and dated 1987 on reverse
pen ink and watercolour with bodycolour
14 ½ x 17 ½ inches

Drawn for an Anglo-American company report

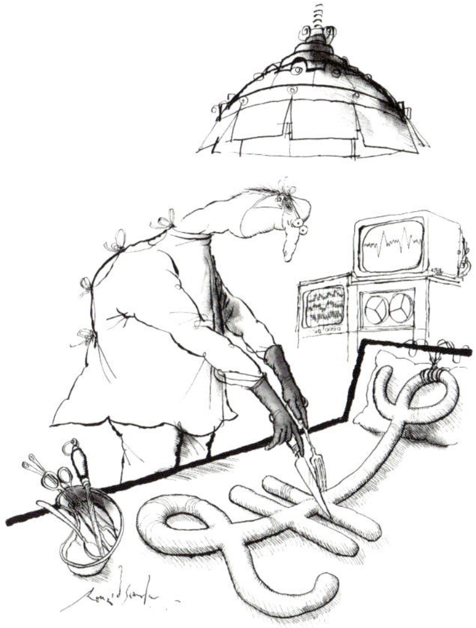

102 CUTTING COSTS
signed
pen and ink
18 x 12 ½ inches

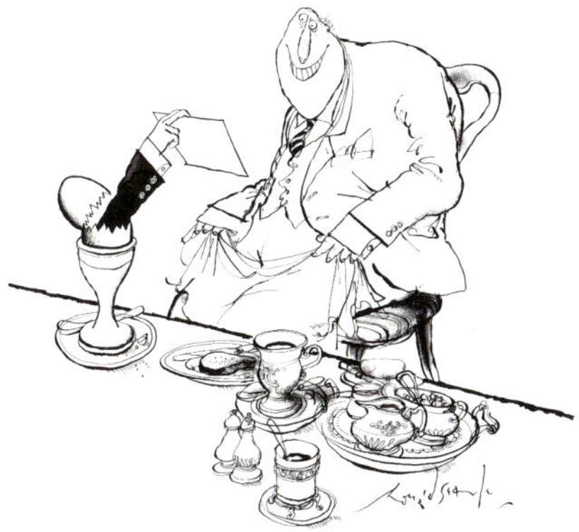

103 THE BRIEFING
signed and inscribed with title
pen and ink with monochrome watercolour
12 x 11 ½ inches

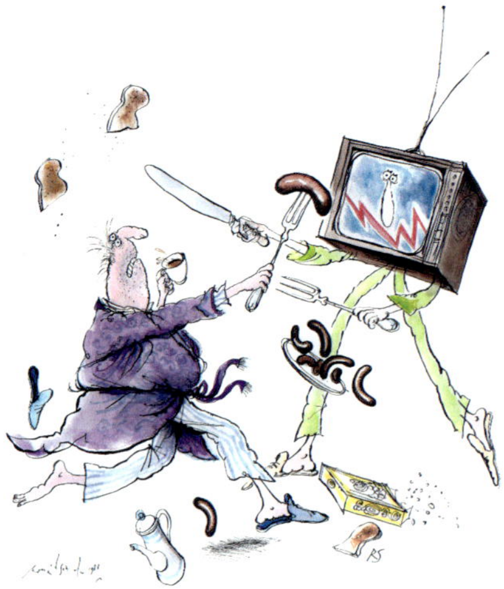

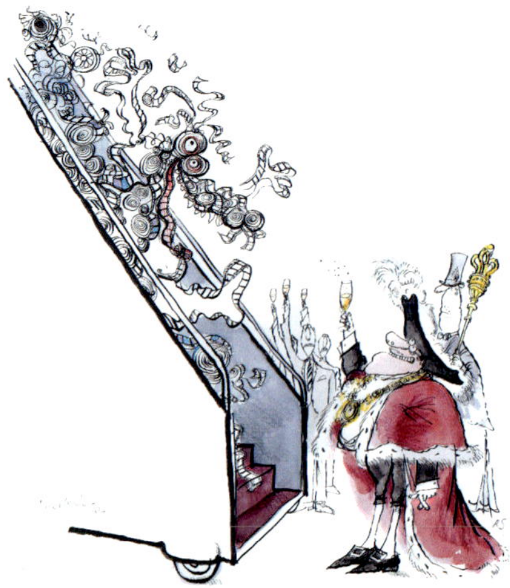

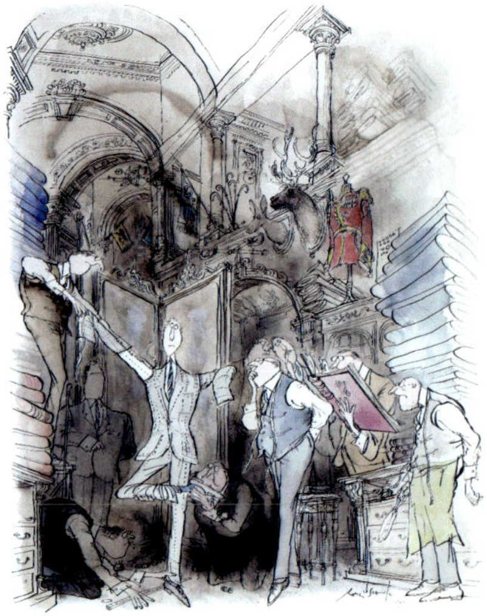

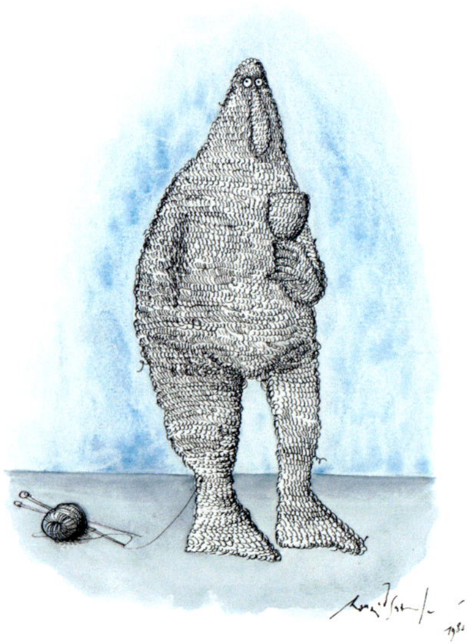

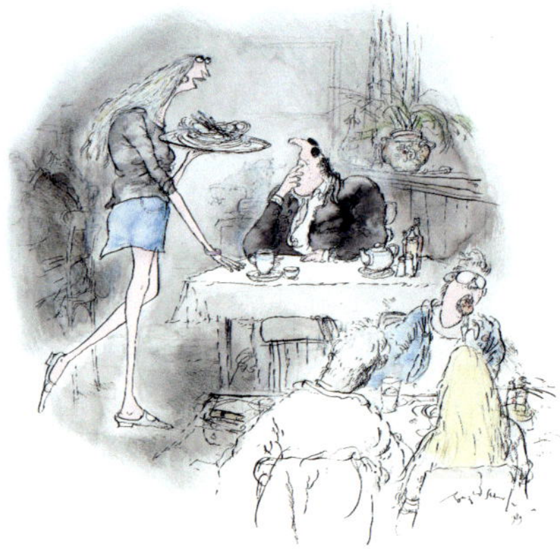

104 BREAKFAST TV
signed, signed with initials, inscribed with title and dated 1983
pen ink and watercolour with crayon
14 x 12 inches
Illustrated: *TV Guide*, New York, 1983

105 WINESPEAK
KNIT TO A HARMONIOUS WHOLE
signed, inscribed with title and dated 1983
pen ink and watercolour
12 ¾ x 9 inches
Illustrated: Ronald Searle, *The Illustrated Winespeak*, London: Souvenir Press, 1983, page 47

106 FILM PUBLICITY:
WELCOME TO A FILM PERSON
signed, inscribed with title and dated 1984
pen ink and watercolour with crayon
14 x 12 ¼ inches
Illustrated: *TV Guide*, New York

107 TEA SHOPPE
signed, inscribed with title and dated 1989
pen ink and watercolour with crayon
15 x 15 ½ inches
Illustrated: *Conde Nast Travel Magazine*, April 1990, 'London' by David Mamet

108 SAVILE ROW IN ALL ITS GLORY
signed, inscribed with title and dated 1989
pen ink and watercolour
19 ¼ x 16 inches
Illustrated: *Town and Country*, New York, April 1989

Numbers 109-114 are all illustrated in *Slightly Foxed – But Still Desirable: Ronald Searle's Wicked World of Book Collecting*, London: Souvenir Press, 1989.

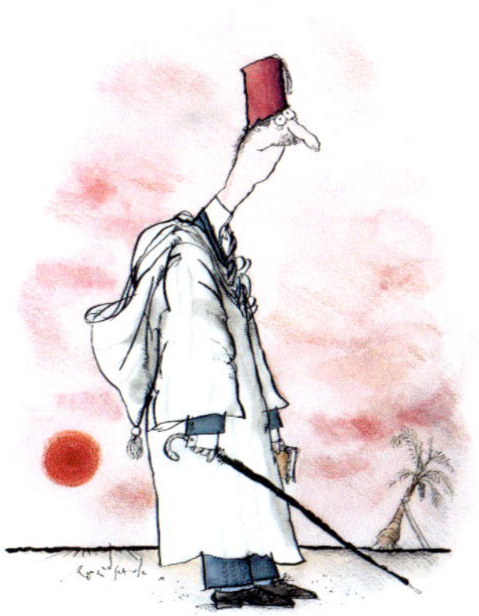

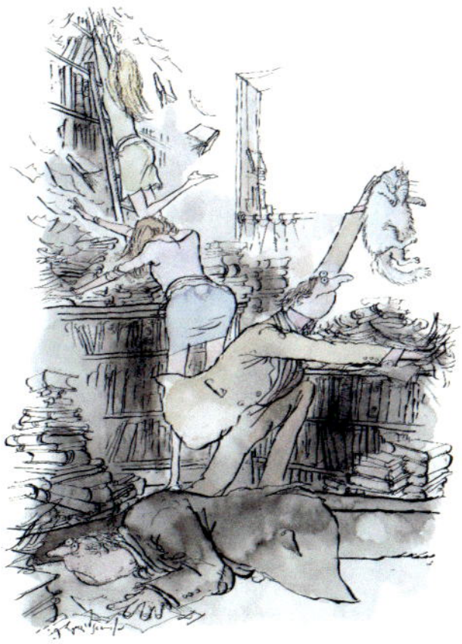

109 PSEUDO – MOROCCO
signed
dated 1989 on reverse
pen ink and watercolour
11 ½ x 9 inches
Illustrated: *Slightly Foxed*, page 83

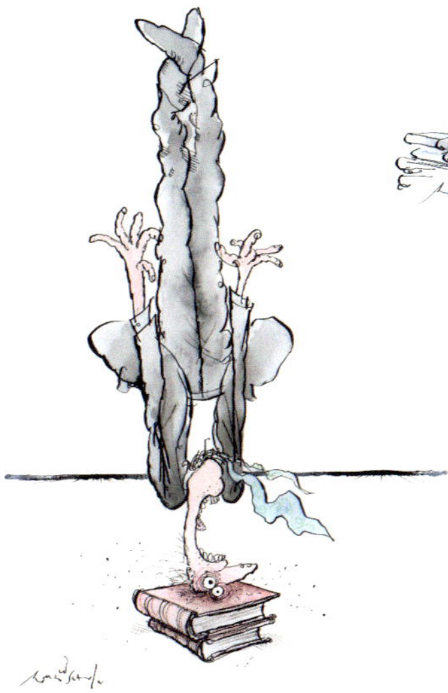

110 NICE SET, BUT ONE VOLUME MISSING
signed, inscribed with title and 'The Wicked World of Bookselling'
pen ink and watercolour
12 ½ x 10 inches
Another version of the same drawing in pen and ink on reverse
Drawn for but not illustrated in *Slightly Foxed*

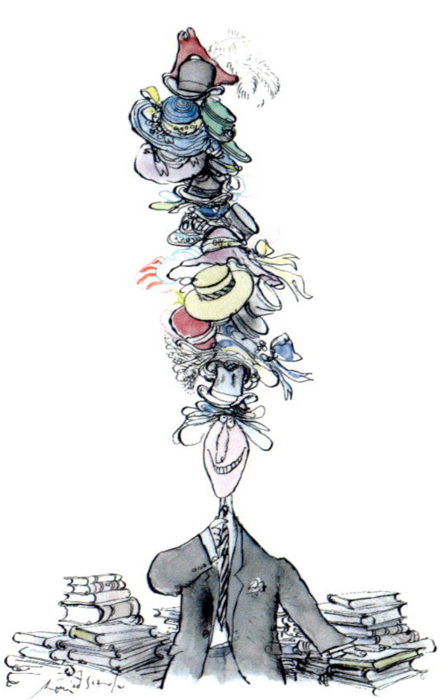

111 NUMEROUS HEADPIECES
signed
pen ink and watercolour with crayon
12 ½ x 9 inches
Illustrated: *Slightly Foxed*, page 49

112 OUTWARDLY CRACKING
signed
pen ink, watercolour and crayon
12 x 9 inches
Illustrated: *Slightly Foxed*, page 39

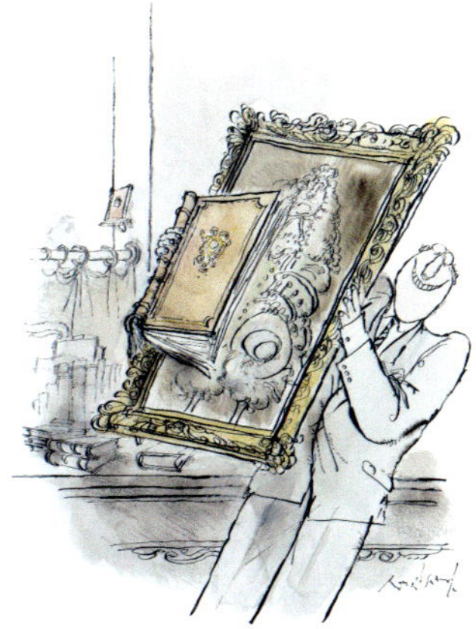

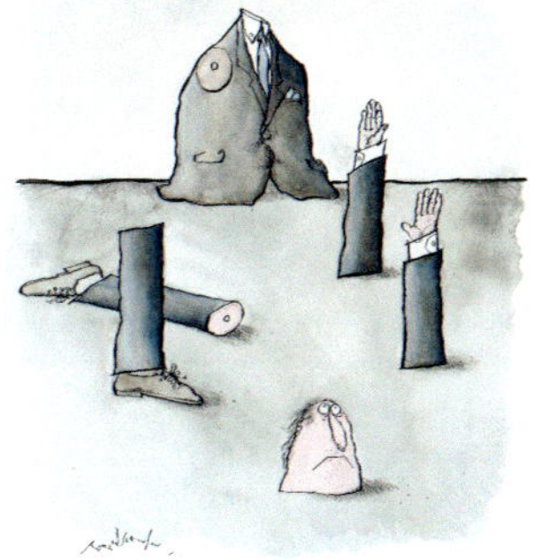

113 ADDED PORTRAIT
signed and inscribed 'The Wicked World of Bookselling'
pen ink and watercolour
12 ½ x 10 inches
Drawn for but not illustrated in *Slightly Foxed*

114 DISBOUND
signed
dated 1989 on reverse
pen ink and watercolour
11 x 9 inches
Illustrated: *Slightly Foxed*, page 45

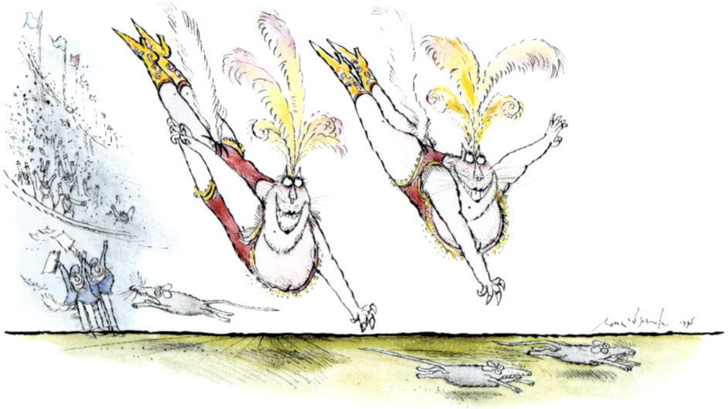

115 SYNCHRONISED RATTING
signed, inscribed with title and dated 1995
pen ink, watercolour and coloured crayon
11 ¼ x 18 ¾ inches

Illustrated: *Delta Sky* (inflight magazine), March 1996
Exhibited: 'Wonderland: an Exhibition of Children's Book Illustrations', Cecil Higgins Art Gallery, Bedford, July-October 2001

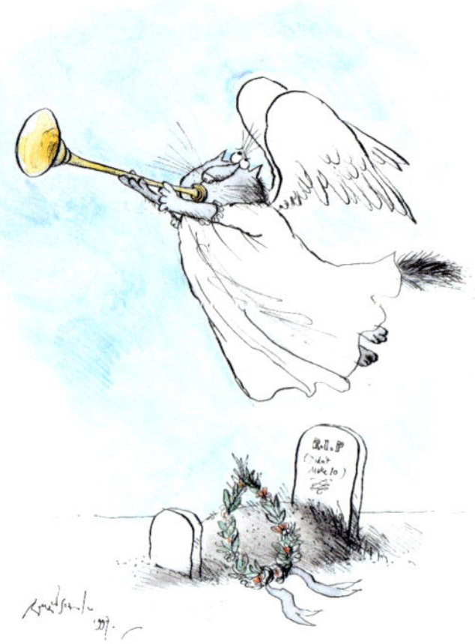

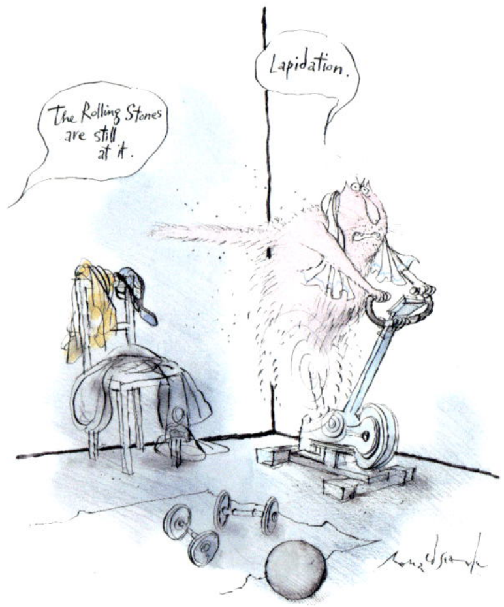

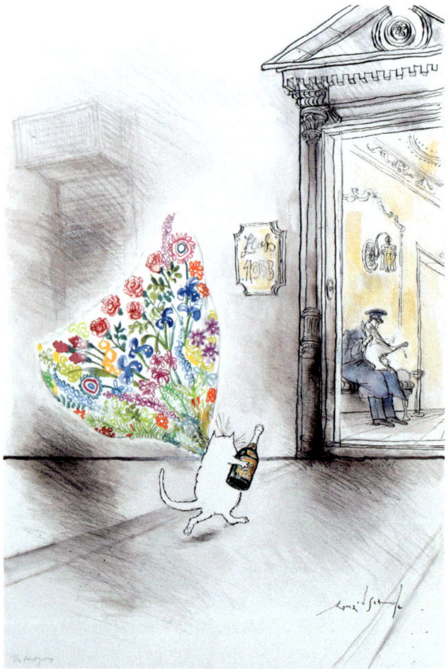

116 THE RENDEZVOUS
signed and inscribed with title
dated 1990 on reverse
watercolour, pen ink and crayon
17 ½ x 12 inches

117 GREAT MOMENTS IN MUSIC
signed and dated 1993
pen ink and watercolour; 14 x 11 ½ inches
Illustrated: *New Yorker*, 1993

118 NINE LIVES – (DIDN'T MAKE TEN)
signed and dated 1997
pen ink and watercolour
13 x 11 ¾ inches

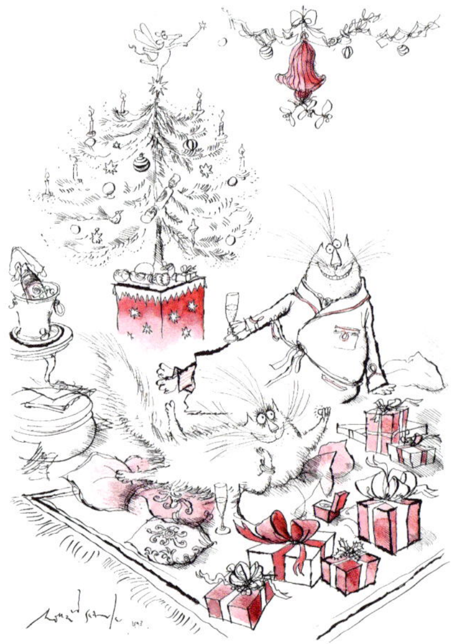

119 CHRISTMAS PRESENTS
signed and dated 1993
inscribed with title, publishing details and dated 1993 on reverse
pen ink, watercolour and crayon
18 ¾ x 14 ¼ inches

Design for a Christmas card for *Married Women* magazine, New York

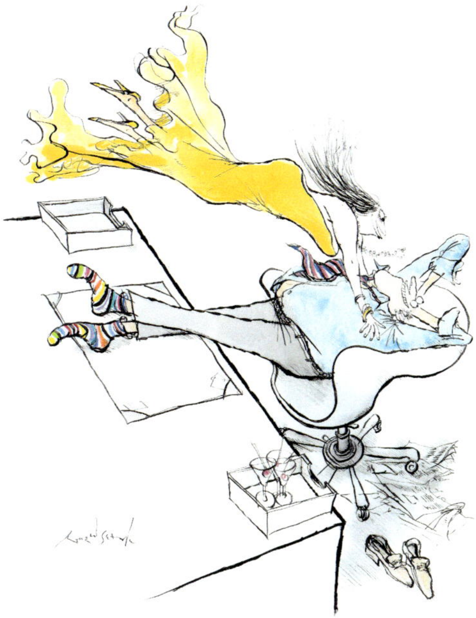

120 WORK BREAK
signed and inscribed with title
inscribed with title and dated 1995
on reverse
watercolour, pen ink and crayon
17 x 14 inches

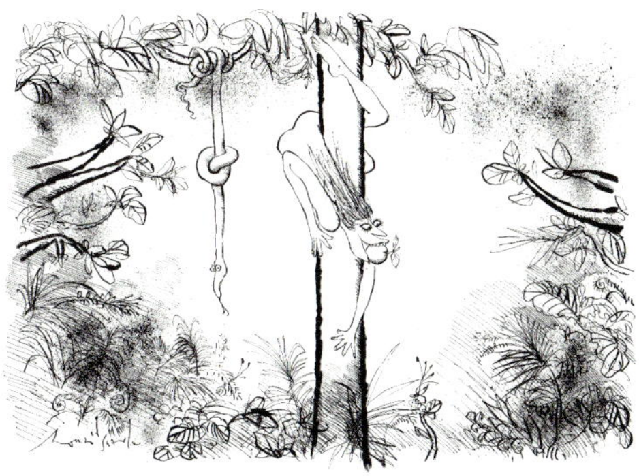

121 POLITICALLY INCORRECT
signed and inscribed with title
inscribed 'first draft of drawing published by Journal Le Monde, Paris, 11 February 1997' and dated 1996 on reverse
pen and ink
13 ½ x 18 ½ inches

Illustrated: *Ronald Searle in Le Monde*, Chicago: University of Chicago Press, 2002, page 83

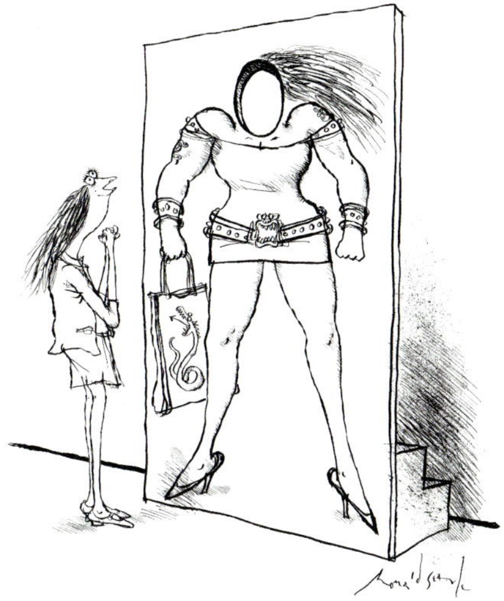

122 GIRLPOWER !
signed
inscribed with publishing details and dated 96 on reverse
inscribed with title and dated 1996 on reverse of original mount board
pen and ink
15 ½ x 13 inches

Illustrated: *International Herald Tribune*, Paris, 16 March 1996, 'Nice & Nasty' by Mary Blume

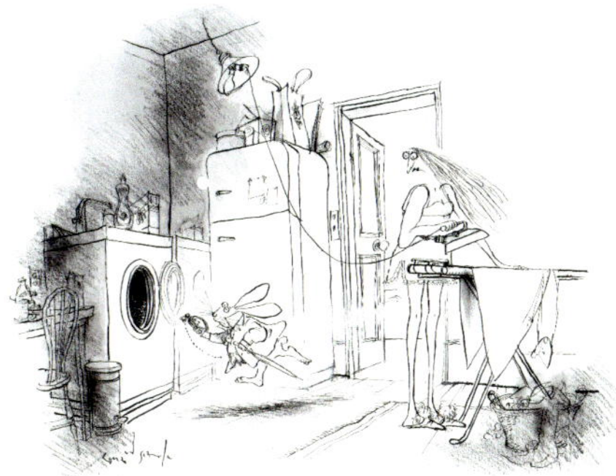

123 ALICE IN NO-MAN'S LAND
signed, inscribed with title and dated 1990
pen ink and crayon
12 ½ x 16 ¾ inches

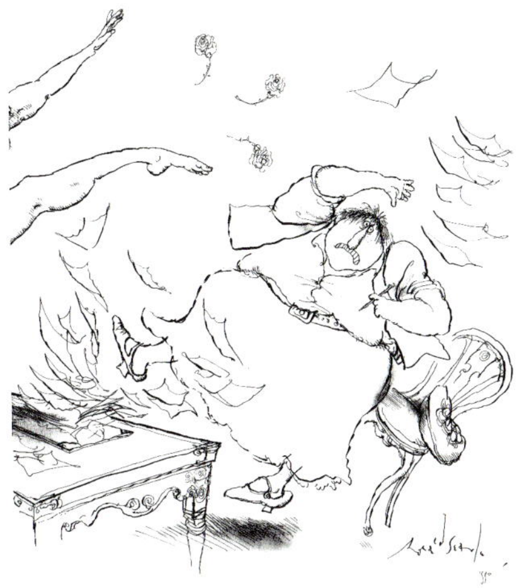

124 BRIEF ENCOUNTERS: GERTRUDE STEIN MEETS SPECTRE DE LA ROSE ROSE ROSE
signed, inscribed with title and dated 1990
pen and ink
13 x 11 ¾ inches

Preliminary drawing for the *New Yorker*, 10 February 1992
Similar to the illustration in Ronald Searle, *Marquis de Sade Meets Goody Two-Shoes*, London: Pavilion, 1994, unpaginated

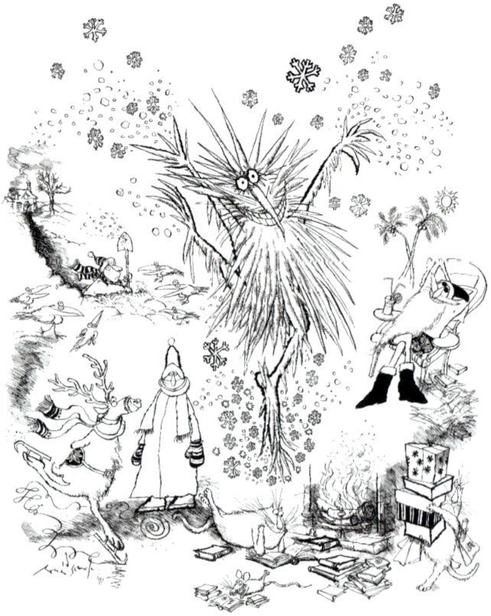

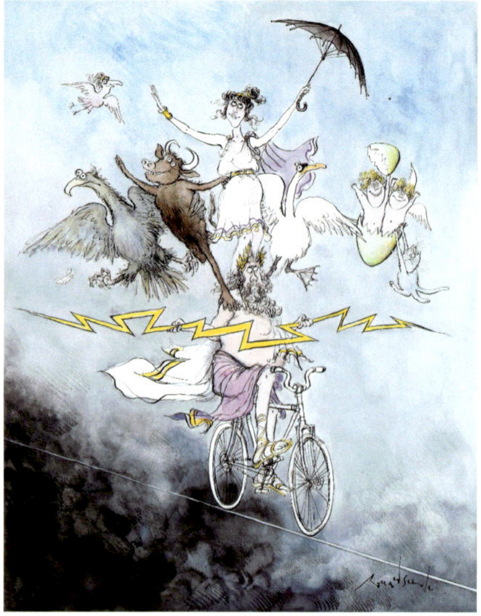

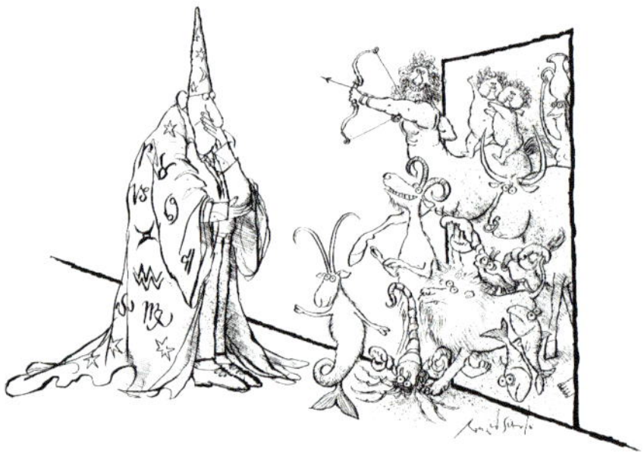

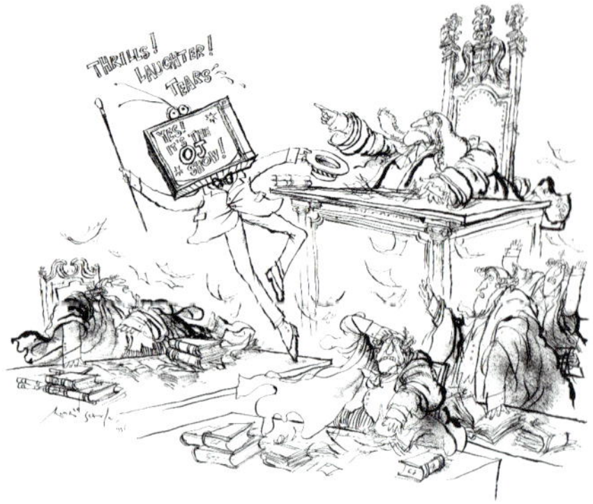

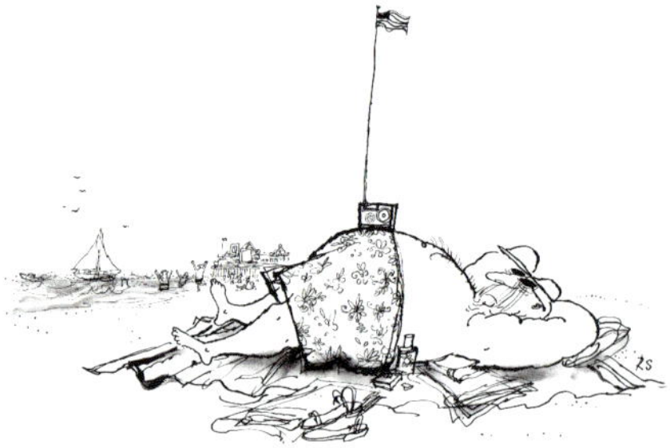

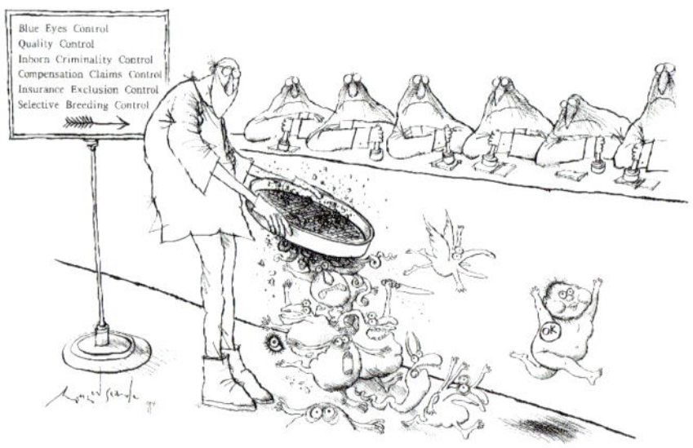

125 WINTER TIME
signed, inscribed with title and dated 1991
pen and ink with pencil
22 x 17 ½ inches
Illustrated: *New York Times*, 15 December 1991

126 ZEUS & CO
signed
inscribed with title below mount
pen ink and watercolour
21 x 16 ½ inches
Illustrated: *Town and Country*, New York, June 1994

127 THE ASTROLOGICAL YEAR: WHAT WILL IT BRING FORTH?
signed and inscribed with title
inscribed with title and dated 1997 on reverse
pen and ink
13 x 17 ½ inches
Illustrated: *International Herald Tribune*, Paris, 27 December 1997, 'Astrologers' by Mary Blume

128 CLONING
signed, inscribed with title and dated 1994
pen and ink
12 x 19 inches
Illustrated: *New York Times*, 4 February 1994

129 FAMOUS TRIALS THAT MIGHT HAVE BEEN THE OJ SHOW HITS GB
signed, inscribed with title and dated 1995
pen and ink
16 ½ x 19 ½ inches
Illustrated: *New York Times*, 2 May 1995, 'Trial of the Vanities' by Frances Fyfield

130 ATLANTIC CITY
signed with initials
pen and ink
9 ½ x 14 inches

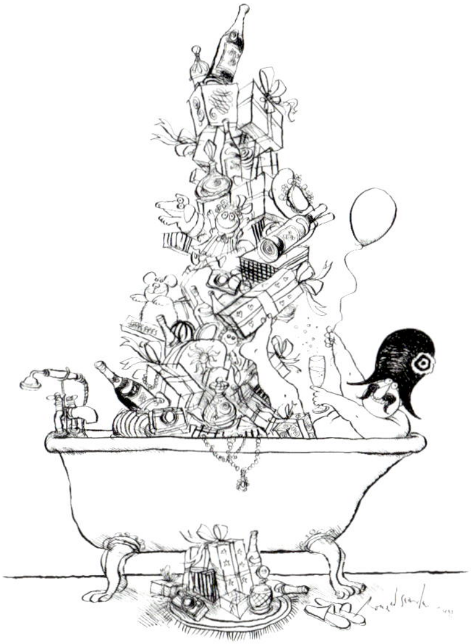

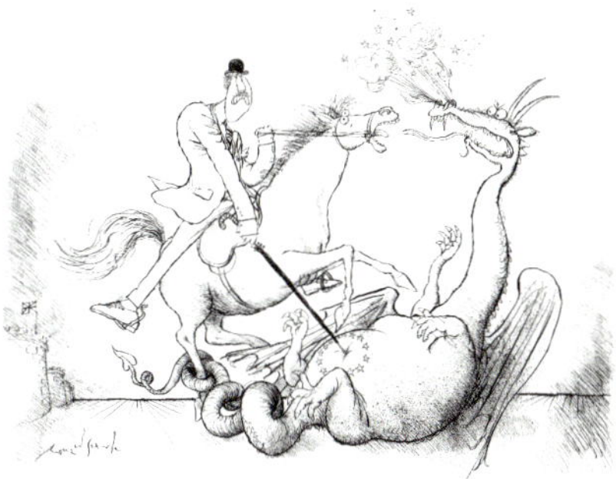

131 L'EUROSCEPTIQUE
signed
inscribed 'St George and Euro Dragon' and dated 1997 on reverse
pen and ink
16 ½ x 19 ¾ inches

Illustrated: *Le Monde*, Paris, 26 March 1997, page 17

Similar to *Ronald Searle in Le Monde*, Chicago: University Press of Chicago, page 29

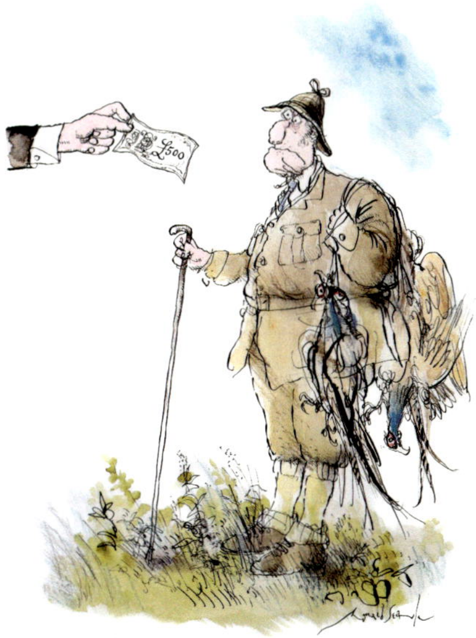

133 GETTIN' THE BIRD
signed and inscribed with title
dated with artist's agent stamp 1991 on reverse
pen ink and watercolour
14 x 10 inches
Pen and ink drawing of a seated man on reverse

132 DAY ACROSS THE CHANNEL
signed, inscribed with title and dated 1997
pen and ink
18 x 15 inches

134 O BEE MYE VALENTYNE
signed, inscribed with title and dated 1992
inscribed with 'For St Valentines day', publishing details and dated 1992 on reverse
pen and ink
21 ¼ x 13 ½ inches

Illustrated: *New York Times*, 14 February 1992

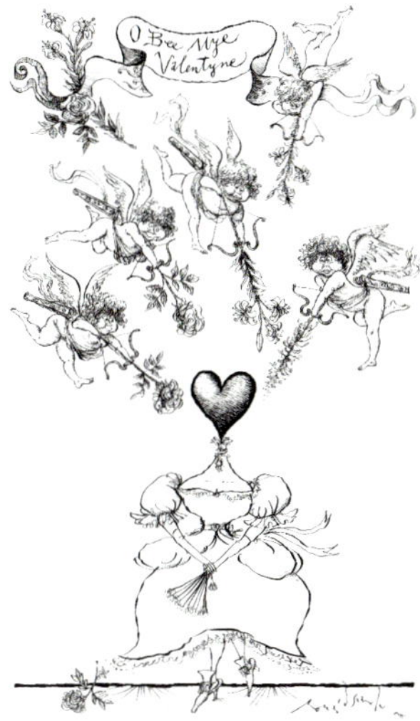

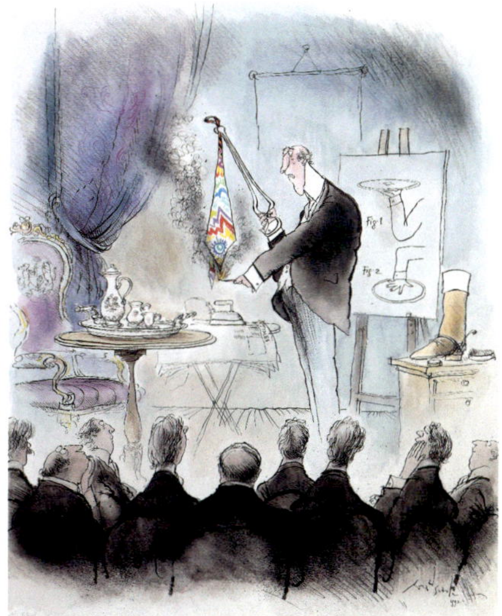

135 BUTLER SCHOOL
signed, inscribed with title and dated 1992
pen ink, watercolour and coloured crayon
19 x 16 inches

Illustrated: *Forbes FYI Magazine*, New York, November 1992

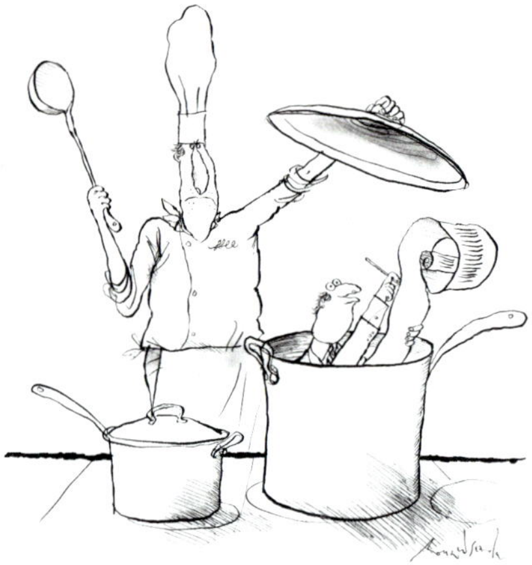

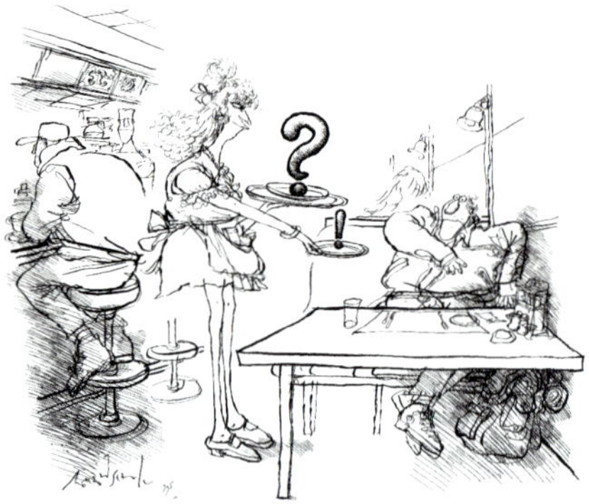

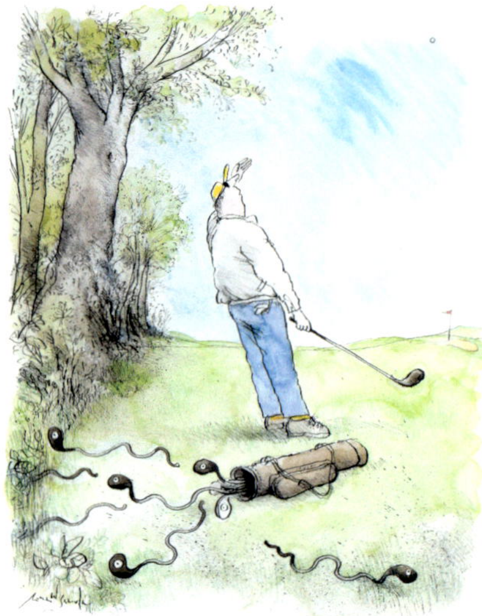

136 ANOTHER DAY, ANOTHER GUIDE
signed and inscribed with title
pen ink and crayon
12 x 12 inches

137 FAST FOOD
signed, inscribed with title and dated 1995
pen and ink
13 ¾ x 15 inches
Illustrated: *International Herald Tribune*, Paris, 14 October 1995, 'Lonely Planet US Phrasebook' by Mary Blume

138 INTO THE ROUGH
signed and inscribed with title
pen ink and watercolour
19 ½ x 16 inches
An illustration for *Into the Rough*, 2000, unpublished

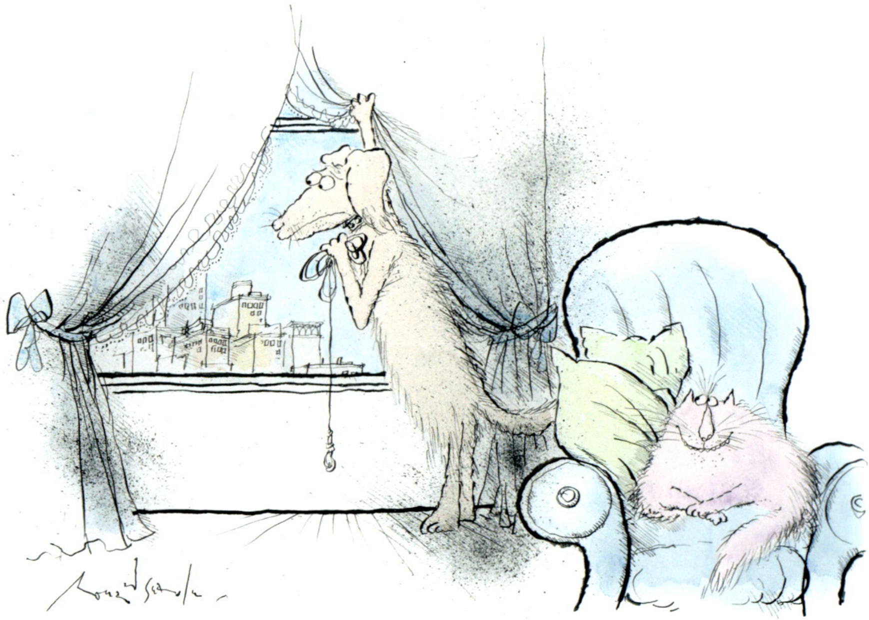

139 WAITING FOR WALKIES
signed and inscribed with title
pen ink and watercolour
12 ¼ x 18 inches
Illustrated: *International Herald Tribune*, Paris, 13 January 2001, 'Ad for Dogwalker' by Mary Blume